SPIRITUALITY: OUR DEEPEST HEART'S DESIRE

Donal Dorr

Spirituality: Our Deepest Heart's Desire

the columba press

First published in 2008 by
the columba press
55A Spruce Avenue, Stillorgan Industrial Park,
Blackrock, Co Dublin

Cover by Bill Bolger
Origination by The Columba Press
Printed in Ireland by ColourBooks Ltd, Dublin

ISBN 978-1-85607-629-6

Achnowledgements

The poem *The Invitation* is taken from the book *THE INVITATION* by Oriah Mountain Dreamer, (c) 1999, published by Harper ONE, San Francisco and Thorsons in the UK. All rights reserved. Presented with permission of the author.

Table of Contents

Introduction

A few months ago I was in South Africa, facilitating a week-long workshop on spirituality for an international group of forty women community animators.[1] Enthused and inspired by the energy and commitment of the group, I woke up in the middle of the night with what was, for me, a new and exciting definition of what spirituality means for me: 'Spirituality, Our Deepest Heart's Desire.' I decided to use that as the title for this book, instead of the more prosaic title I had intended to use.

For many of the people with whom I work, spirituality, in one form or another, is indeed their deepest heart's desire. I know, of course that many other people are so preoccupied with earning a living and looking after their family that spirituality seems to have a secondary—perhaps even a marginal—place in their lives. It might seem, then, that their deepest heart's desire is focused on matters that are much more practical and immediate than spiritual experiences and moral values. Nevertheless, I believe that behind all these immediate practical preoccupations lies a hunger for some richer and deeper meaning and purpose. Indeed I believe that, for most people, spirituality, though it may not be uppermost in their everyday concerns, nevertheless occupies a place deep within them where it underpins much of their actions; and that in their more reflective moments they would wish to be in on-going touch with that spirituality. So I feel that the title of this book is appropriate for them too.

If the title of the book is to be widely applicable, it is necessary to take the word 'spirituality' in quite a broad sense. That is what I have done in this book. In my view, spirituality has two aspects. On the one hand, it refers to our deep longing and searching for meaning, for peace, and for a sense of our personal

---

1. See http://www.tft.org.za/

call and of our 'place in the family of things'[2] as well as our fundamental commitments, mindsets, and attitudes to life. On the other hand, it also includes the various moral, political, or religious activities through which we endeavour to answer our call and to live out our commitments from day to day.

When we look at the latter aspect – the spiritual activities in which we engage – there appears to be an unfortunate split between two quite different approaches. For many people, the word 'spirituality' suggests activities that are very inward-looking, perhaps Buddhist in style. The deepest heart's desire of these people is to achieve personal mindfulness and serenity. At its best this approach can be richly mystical. But, at worst, it can be unduly self-centred, showing little concern for the major social issues of our world; and it may have some of the less attractive aspects of 'New Age' ideas.

There are other people whose spiritual activities are more outward-oriented. The deepest heart's desire of at least some of these people is to ensure that human rights of people all over the world are respected, and that social justice and care for the environment take a central place in the way our world is organised. For them, the word 'spirituality' relates primarily to their efforts to ensure that individuals, communities, and nations can live together in security and peace – and that humanity as a whole can develop and flourish.

My aim in this book is to help people to avoid this split between two approaches to spirituality. I believe that all of us need a rounded spirituality which embraces the best of both senses of the word. We need to look both inward and outward. We need deep spiritual experiences but we also need profound moral commitment. Each of the two dimensions supports the other.

This linking of the moral aspect with the more conventionally 'spiritual' aspect has been an important theme for me throughout my life. I was born into a traditionally pious family where the two aspects were inextricably woven together. My mother had a deep sense of the presence of God and at the same time she devoted much of her energy to helping homeless 'travelling people'. Prayer was central in the life of my father, and he was

---

2. Mary Oliver's poem 'Wild Geese'

deeply concerned about moral matters– including the controversial and politically-charged issue of workers' participation in the management of the factory where he worked. It is not surprising then that my own life and my writings should echo these twofold interests and concerns of my parents.

In all of my books, including the present one, I have drawn on my own direct experiences, to such an extent that the books have been largely an articulation of what has been happening in my life. As I look back over the past forty years of my life's journey, the most striking thing has been the way in which these two aspects of spirituality have been interwoven with each other.

In the early 1970s, while I was working in Africa, the charismatic renewal was inviting Christians to move from a rather intellectual and arid approach to faith to one that was vibrantly alive at the experiential level. This was an important influence on my ministry and on my personal life. It was linked, in my case, with the rediscovery of the original Ignatian spirituality, which puts so much emphasis on religious experience and movements of the Spirit. It was out of this background that I wrote my first book, *Remove the Heart of Stone*, published just thirty years ago.

In the latter half of the 1970s I became deeply engaged in training community activists who were involved in struggling for social justice and liberation. This on-the-ground experience inspired me to devote time to a study of development economics and related topics – and to a detailed examination of Catholic social teaching on these issues. My concern for the more political aspects of spirituality found expression in *Option for the Poor*, first published in 1983 and revised and expanded in 1992. In *Spirituality and Justice* (1984) I attempted to bring together the two themes of personal and political-social spirituality.

My on-going work with groups of socially and politically committed Christians, at home and abroad, led me to write two further books. The first of these, *Integral Spirituality* (1990), was a practical resource-book, dealing with both the personal and political aspects of spirituality. The second, *The Social Justice Agenda* (1991) was my attempt to offer a succinct and ecumenical presentation of Christian social teaching and thinking, written at a popular level.

From the mid-1990s onwards, I began to do fewer workshops on social justice issues and devoted more time to workshops related mainly to personal spiritual development. This led me, in *Divine Energy* (1996) to focus mostly on the more personal aspects of spirituality, interpreting the role of Jesus and the Holy Spirit in ways that can be experienced in the everyday lives of ordinary people. All during the 1990s, however, I acted as a resource-person for the Irish Missionary Union; and this work led to *Mission in Today's World* (2000), where I returned again to the more public dimension of spirituality. Four years later, in *Time for a Change*, I moved over and back between the personal-contemplative and the active-political aspects.

Over the past ten years I have run dozens of workshops with the leadership teams of a variety of religious congregations and with teams of social workers. *Spirituality of Leadership* (2006) comes out of this experience. In it I emphasised again the links between the political and the personal aspects of spirituality – this time with a focus on the exercise of leadership.

In the present book I am once more attempting to bring out the close relationship between the personal and the social-political. But on this occasion I have adopted a different approach. In the first part of the book I suggest that a wide variety of moral values find an underpinning in personal and interpersonal spiritual experiences which are quite common in our world. Some examples of the kind of experiences which I have in mind are falling in love, or giving birth to a child, or reconciling with a friend. I call them spiritual experiences because they touch people at a very deep level and can change their lives. These spiritual experiences are by no means confined to Christians. They are universal.

I believe it is important to begin an exploration of spirituality by looking at these universally available experiences, because many of the spiritual 'searchers' of our world are disillusioned with the church, or even with all forms of organised religion. Furthermore, many Christian believers have become spiritually jaded or flat, finding themselves bored or not adequately nourished by what the churches are offering them at present. My hope is that they may find renewed faith and energy by looking more deeply at 'secular' experiences whose spiritual dimension they may not have fully appreciated. In the later chapters of the first part of the book (chapters 4, 5, and 6), I go on to offer a more explicitly Christian interpretation of the mystery which lies behind these experiences.

The second part of the book is more biblical in approach. It delves into the notion of a very personal call – from God, or from 'the Beyond'. It does so by exploring the calls of six figures from the bible, three men and three women, beginning with Abraham and ending with Mary, the mother of Jesus. My aim in this exploration is to throw light on the personal call of each one of us, a call which lies at the heart of each person's spiritual journey.

In the third and final part of the book I spell out in more practical detail the relationship between morality and spirituality. The eight chapters in this section are devoted to a spirituality of intimacy, an ecological spirituality, a spirituality of human rights, a spirituality of social justice, a spirituality of liberation and reconciliation, and what I am calling 'a spirituality for sellers and buyers'. In this part, as in the earlier parts, my aim is to put forward a rounded spirituality, one which takes seriously both the personal contemplative aspect and the more active moral and political aspects.

Throughout the book I have attempted to stay true to my title in which I suggest that the source of our spirituality is our deepest heart's desire. My hope is that the book may be of some help even to those for whom spirituality is not obviously at the top of their immediate concerns. They may see it as an invitation to get in touch with the deeper longing of their hearts. I believe they can do so if they take time to reflect on such everyday but profound experiences as being forgiven, or being loved unconditionally by a friend, or sensing a call from 'beyond' to devote their life to another person or to some worthwhile cause; and also if they reflect on their concern about the injustice and oppression which are rampant in our world.

As I draw this introduction to a close I want to note that this is not primarily a 'how-to' book about spirituality. By this I mean that I have not set out to propose various exercises or practices by which we can foster our spirituality. My concern here has been with the content of spirituality rather than with techniques.

I note also that in this book I have not made any attempt to deal with the sacramental life, even though the Eucharist is a central feature in my own spirituality. My focus has been on what I believe lies behind the sacraments and the other distinctive aspects of church life. I believe that sacraments become mere empty rituals unless they are underpinned by deep spiritual experiences which can put us in touch with the mystery which surrounds our lives. The reason why many people at this time do not find the sacramental rituals very life-giving is, I believe, that they are not sufficiently aware of the depth and spiritual quality of some of the everyday events and encounters in their lives. My aim in this book is to invite readers to explore such spiritual experiences and the deep moral commitments to which they are linked.

I take this opportunity to express my appreciation and gratitude to my friend Padraig Ó Máille and my brother Noel Dorr for their detailed and comprehensive critique of an earlier draft of this work, and to Jean Eason and Noel Bradley for their helpful suggestions on key points.

Donal Dorr, August 2008

PART I

Spiritual Experiences and Moral Values

… God is not all
In one place, complete
… God is in the bits and pieces of Everyday –
A kiss here and a laugh again, and sometimes tears,
A pearl necklace round the neck of poverty.[1]

The Invitation
by Oriah Mountain Dreamer

It doesn't interest me what you do for a living.
I want to know what you ache for
and if you dare to dream of meeting your heart's longing.

It doesn't interest me how old you are.
I want to know if you will risk looking like a fool
for love
for your dream
for the adventure of being alive.

It doesn't interest me what planets are squaring your moon...
I want to know if you have touched the centre of your own
sorrow
if you have been opened by life's betrayals
or have become shrivelled and closed
from fear of further pain.

I want to know if you can sit with pain
mine or your own
without moving to hide it
or fade it
or fix it.

I want to know if you can be with joy
mine or your own

---

1. Patrick Kavanagh, 'The Great Hunger', in *The Complete Poems*, Goldsmith Press, Newbridge, 1988, p 88.

if you can dance with wildness
and let the ecstasy fill you to the tips of your fingers and toes
without cautioning us
to be careful
to be realistic
to remember the limitations of being human.

It doesn't interest me if the story you are telling me is true.
I want to know if you can
disappoint another
to be true to yourself.
If you can bear the accusation of betrayal
and not betray your own soul.
If you can be faithless
and therefore trustworthy.

I want to know if you can see Beauty
even when it is not pretty
every day.
And if you can source your own life
from its presence.

I want to know if you can live with failure
yours and mine
and still stand at the edge of the lake
and shout to the silver of the full moon,
"Yes."

It doesn't interest me
to know where you live or how much money you have.
I want to know if you can get up
after the night of grief and despair
weary and bruised to the bone
and do what needs to be done
to feed the children.

It doesn't interest me who you know
or how you came to be here.
I want to know if you will stand
in the centre of the fire
with me
and not shrink back.

It doesn't interest me where or what or with whom
you have studied.
I want to know what sustains you
from the inside
when all else falls away.

I want to know if you can be alone
with yourself
and if you truly like the company you keep
in the empty moments.

CHAPTER ONE

Interpersonal Spiritual Experiences

In this chapter I propose to look at a variety of experiences – ones which I am calling 'spiritual' because they can have a significant and often a transforming effect in a person's life. The lives of many of us are so busy, and we are so preoccupied by a succession of immediate concerns, that we can easily fail to advert to such spiritual experiences – or at least fail to give them the full attention they deserve. If this is the pattern of our lives we will find ourselves living on the surface of life, seldom or never getting in touch with what brings us a surge of joy, hope, and new energy, or a sense that life is meaningful, worthwhile, and has a purpose. We will not find within us the desire to reach out in love and sympathy to others. We will not experience that sense of outrage which would impel us to challenge the gross evils in the world around us.

If we fail to open ourselves to a whole variety of everyday spiritual experiences, we can scarcely expect to have any deep experience of God. For, adapting the lines of Kavanagh's poem quoted above, we could say that God is behind and beyond our everyday spiritual experiences and they offer us an opening into an experience of God.

Furthermore, I want to argue that such spiritual experiences provide an underpinning for ethical values and virtues and genuine moral commitment. One of the major problems in our modern Western or westernised world is a growing absence of any secure basis for morality. In the past, morality was so closely linked with religion that few people made any clear distinction between the two. But in some parts of the world today people have become disenchanted with religion in general. More widely still, many people have begun to question aspects of the religion they were brought up with as children. Moral values have become detached, to a considerable extent, from religious beliefs.

This raises considerable difficulty for those who wish to incul-
cate moral behaviour in children or to promote moral commitment in adults.

It is particularly difficult to promote the kind of strong effective moral action which is required to protect the environment or
to overcome the massive social injustices of our present-day
world. Some people – perhaps relatively few – may say 'why
bother?' But far more will acknowledge the problems and the
need for decisive action but will fail to find the energy to do anything about them. There is a kind of hopelessness, mixed in with
a vague feeling of guilt, which makes people bury their heads in
the sand rather than being galvanised into action.

The most effective way which I can envisage to break out of
this paralysis is to invite and encourage people to really 'let in'
the kind of spiritual experiences which are available to anybody
who is open to them. I believe that these experiences, once they
are allowed to touch people at a deep heart level, provide a secure
and energy-filled basis for moral values and moral commitment.
I hope to illustrate this point by noting a wide variety of the kind
of spiritual experiences which I have in mind.

Love

One deeply spiritual experience is that of falling in love. The
person who is in love feels much more fully alive, no longer living in the drab everyday world. Life has taken on a richer and
deeper meaning. One looks with new eyes at other people – and
above all at the person with whom one is in love. Those who are
in love feel lifted out of their preoccupation with themselves.
They find themselves instead thinking spontaneously of what
will please the other rather than of their own self-interest. And
all this takes place not because the person has planned it. Rather
it is something that happens to one – a gift that comes at times
more or less against one's will.

Closely related to this experience is the feeling of being loved
unconditionally – loved not because one has earned that love
but simply for one's own sake. Once again this can be a transforming experience. It sets one free from the nagging doubt that
whispers in one's ear, saying, 'You are not good enough', or
'You have not done enough', or 'If others really knew what you

are like they would reject you.' There is an interesting contrast here: falling in love inclines a person to reach out to the other; but knowing one is fully loved is more an experience of resting in that love, basking in it. For many of us it can be quite difficult to let in that experience fully and to stay in it.

Childbirth and Parenthood

In my workshops on spirituality I have found that one of the deepest spiritual experiences for many women is that of giving birth to a child. Some women are a little slow to mention this. It is almost as though they did not expect anybody to believe them – and this can mean that they have not fully acknowledged it even to themselves. But, once the experience is named, it evokes an immediate response – and at times a very moving sharing of how profoundly it has affected them.

In more recent times it has become common for men to be present while their partners are giving birth. This allows them to share to a considerable extent in the wonder and joy of the childbirth experience. Indeed all of us can have some significant sharing in this experience when we look with love on a newborn infant.

Childbirth is just the first stage in the on-going adventure of parenthood. As a child grows up, its parents go through a whole gamut of experiences. At times there is deep pain, anger and distress. On other occasions there is pride and joy. The whole journey of parenting is never one that allows them to be neutral or indifferent. Once they have a child the whole pattern of the lives of the parents is radically changed for perhaps twenty years. Even when their children have grown up and have moved elsewhere the parents still find themselves preoccupied with their welfare. All this is a deeply spiritual experience, engaging the parents at a most profound level and transforming their conception of what life is about and of what they find truly important in life.

Healing

Yet another deeply spiritual experience for many people is that of being healed. We can be wounded or hurt or damaged in many different ways. So our healing may be of the body, or of the mind, or of the spirit. Whatever form it comes in, healing often restores purpose and energy and new life to the person. Some of the deepest and most spiritual experiences of healing are from addictions or depression.

Forgiveness

There can also be a healing of one's relationship with another person, or with a whole community. It comes in the form of forgiving and being forgiven. This too can transform a person's life, changing the way one looks at others and at oneself. It brings a spiritual freedom which energises and opens up a new perspective on others and on life.

Most of us find it difficult to forgive others. Real forgiveness may take a long time in coming to us. When it eventually comes, it is often experienced as a gift or grace, rather than as something we have achieved by our own efforts.

For some of us the hardest thing is not so much to forgive others as to allow ourselves to be forgiven by them. We find it difficult to let in the gift of forgiveness; perhaps we feel we do not deserve it. Furthermore, we may find it hard to forgive ourselves – and we get into a downward spiral where we cannot forgive ourselves for being slow to forgive others or ourselves. W. B. Yeats had a keen awareness of the importance of forgiving ourselves. This is the final verse of his poem 'A Dialogue of Self and Soul':

> I am content to follow to its source
> Every event in action, or in thought;
> Measure the lot; forgive myself the lot!
> When such as I cast out remorse
> So great a sweetness flows into the breast
> We must laugh and we must sing,
> We are blest by everything,
> Everything we look upon is blest.[1]

It is important to keep reminding ourselves that forgiveness – of ourselves or others – is always a gift, not something we can earn. It is only when we really experience this sense of being gifted and graced that our relationship with God can become

1. *Collected Poems of W. B. Yeats*, London (Macmillan: 1963) p 267.

close and genuine. This experience of grace lies at the heart of what it means to be a Christian. Indeed we may add that it is also at the heart of what it means to be fully human.

Community

One aspect of the change in Western culture brought about some three centuries ago by the Enlightenment is that people came to have a much keener awareness of themselves as individuals, not just as part of a larger society. Unfortunately, there is a 'flip side' to that development: we have a much weaker sense of community and so we often feel isolated, lonely, even lost.

In these circumstances it can be a powerful spiritual experience to feel oneself part of a caring and sharing community. The sense of being part of a community may come in a variety of ways. It is often experienced quite strongly when people gather round to comfort us as we mourn the loss of a loved one. In a lighter mode it may come when we experience ourselves as part of a county or province or country celebrating a great victory in a sporting event.

In Ireland, many people had a deeply moving experience of being part of a wider community when the Good Friday Agreement of 1998 brought a sense that peace had come to Northern Ireland. In the USA the terrorist attack of 'nine-eleven' evoked a quite extraordinary sense of community among people all over America and indeed elsewhere in the world. This seemed to be one of those rare and special occasions when people all over the world felt themselves part of a community. Perhaps other such moments were when Nelson Mandela walked free from prison, or the time when a tsunami wiped out hundreds of thousands of people in Asia.

Participation

When the experience of community occurs in the context of practical action it can give rise to a profoundly spiritual experience of participation. This gives us the sense that we are actively involved in shaping the future of a movement, of a country, and even perhaps of the wider world. When we participate actively in the development of some local community or organisation – or in articulating the vision, the direction and mission-statement of a religious congregation – we have a sense of being truly respected, of ownership of the process. We feel that our voices have been heard and taken account of in the making of the key decisions.

When the experience of participation takes place in a more overtly political context it brings energy and new life into politics. Then freshness and enthusiasm replace the sense of futility, suspicion and cynicism which so many people feel nowadays in relation to politicians and to any kind of political activity.

Reconciliation
Closely related to the experience of forgiveness and of community is that of reconciliation. In relationships between individuals, families and small communities, reconciliation involves two-way forgiveness. Quite frequently it brings a new warmth and depth into people's relationships with each other.

In the political sphere, on the other hand, reconciliation often entails something both less and more than forgiveness. It may involve something *less* than full personal forgiveness, since it is more a matter of a willingness of former enemies to keep their resentment and grievances under control while they work together for the common good. It is *more* than personal forgiveness in the sense that the focus is mainly on the future – on an undertaking on both sides to co-operate in the interests of the wider society. A recent striking example is the close working relationship built up in Northern Ireland between Revd Ian Paisley, who was formerly known mainly for saying 'no' to all peace plans, and Martin McGuinness former head of the IRA.

The Experience of Evil
At first sight it may seem strange to name the experience of evil as a spiritual experience. But a 'spiritual' experience in the sense we are considering here is any event which touches us at a very deep level and may have a transforming effect in our lives. And for many people this occurs when they come up close to some serious natural disaster such as an earthquake or a devastating hurricane.

Something that can and should touch us even more deeply is to let in the reality of a serious moral evil, such as genocide, torture, or the use of rape as an instrument of war. Indeed I would go so far as to say that our spiritual understanding remains shallow if we fail to acknowledge the reality of moral evil. And this acknowledgement needs to be not just a notional or intellectual one; we must also allow it to pierce us at the heart level.

Moral Values and Virtues
When I refer here to a moral value I mean simply whatever it is that makes us judge an action or behaviour to be good and morally worthwhile, something that ought to be respected and chosen. When a person develops a pattern of behaviour which puts such a moral value into practice and a certain facility in acting in this way, we can say that this person is virtuous or is practising a virtue. I want to suggest that our commitment to moral values and our development of virtues will be fostered if we advert to, and appreciate, the kind of spiritual experiences I am describing in this chapter. If, on the other hand, we pay little attention to our spiritual experiences then our adherence to moral values and virtues is likely to be vague and notional.

The spiritual experiences of love, of community, of participation, of evil, of healing and of reconciliation give us a solid basis for a variety of moral values and virtues. The experience of loving and being loved invites us to reach out to others with respect and with genuine concern for problems they may be having. When this reaching out takes place on a one-to-one basis, or in a family or small community, it has a quality of gentleness, even tenderness.

The moral virtue of fidelity also finds a foundation in the experience of loving and being loved. For one has personal evidence that genuine love is not something that is 'here today and gone tomorrow'. It is patient and tenacious, marked by a willingness to 'hang in there' through thick and thin.

For many people it is the experience of parenting which gives them their deepest sense of the importance of fidelity. There are times when their children stretch their patience and endurance almost to breaking-point. But part of being a parent is finding that parents can never give up. Their love and concern for the welfare of the child compels them to remain faithful and committed, in order to see the child through. This experience is particularly powerful in the case of parents of 'special children' – those who are mentally or physically disabled.

In the larger political context of a whole country, the value and virtue of patriotism is grounded in the experience of belonging to community and of solidarity with others. And nowadays we feel ourselves invited to extend this patriotism outwards so that it is no longer limited by national boundaries. Already in Europe there is need for a commitment to the well-being of the European Union as a whole as well as of all the other countries with which it has ever-expanding links and relationships. In our more optimistic moments we may see some indications – or believe there are realistic hopes – that this more extended form of patriotism is beginning to develop in Europe in somewhat the same way as it developed in America as the United States moved from being a set of isolated colonies and states to becoming a single nation which could embrace a wide diversity of peoples and cultures.

As we now face the reality of living in 'a global village' the next step that is required is a major expansion of the virtue of humanitarian solidarity and concern. Already dozens of states and millions of people all over the world have begun to respond to this newly urgent moral value. In times of disaster or emergency people's concern arises, at best, from an empathy with the suffering of others – one that is not marred by a paternalistic attitude or a desire to impress others.

It is arguable that what sets people free to adopt such a generous and altruistic love for others is their own awareness of being loved and knowing that they are lovable. This personal experience of love animates their empathetic distress on behalf of those who are suffering and their efforts to relieve this suffering.

There are many situations where a person's concern may be combined with righteous anger about abuses, injustice, and oppression, and ecological damage. It is here that we find the relevance of the spiritual experience of acknowledging the reality of evil. That awareness of evil combines with people's experiences of community and love. Together they provide a solid spiritual basis for commitment to struggle for liberation, for social justice, as well as for respect for fundamental human rights and for the environment.

One of the most important of all human rights is the right to participate – to have an effective 'say' in decisions that concern us both at the local level and in the wider political world. For, by exercising this right, people can work with others to create a society where other fundamental rights are respected. And the commitment to gaining and protecting the right to participate is nourished by one's previous positive experiences of participation in various organisations. So, here once again, is a situation where a moral value and virtue is underpinned by the kind of spiritual experiences we have been considering.

What about the experiences of forgiveness and reconciliation? These, too, provide a basis for vitally important moral values and virtues. When we feel forgiven and reconciled with others we sense at once that we have come in touch with experiences that are central to what it means to be truly human. This constitutes an invitation to give a significant place in our lives to the values of forgiveness and reconciliation. We respond by committing ourselves to be people who devote much of our energy to working for reconciliation in our families, our communities, and in the wider society. We experience the truth of the words of the gospel: 'Blessed are the peacemakers.' (Mt 5:9)

CHAPTER TWO

Personal Spiritual Experiences

A Call

So far I have been dealing with a range of spiritual experiences involving our relationships with others. It is time now to move on to experiences that touch us more in our purely personal lives.

Many people have the experience of feeling a personal call to take on a particular way of life or some important task. This call can come in different forms. To some people it comes, as it did to Abraham and Moses, as a conviction that they are experiencing a personal call from a God with whom they are in active dialogue. For others it can come in the form of an invitation or challenge from the people with whom they are in solidarity; that is the way the bible describes the call that came to Esther.

Nowadays, people sometimes experience it, as Judith in the bible did, in the form of a firm belief that the authorities are making a disastrously wrong choice which can only be remedied or challenged by taking on some heroic personal action.[1] More commonly, the call comes as a strong personal attraction – a kind of inner invitation – to take up a particular task or way of life. But, whatever form it takes, it can be a deep experience – one which gives purpose and meaning to the person's life. In that sense we can call it a *spiritual* experience, even if the person does not believe in a personal God.

The spiritual experience of feeling called to a way of life or a particular task can provide a foundation for a number of closely-related values and virtues. These include *docility* and *obedience* – not in the sense of being weak and spineless but rather in the sense of being willing to follow the call generously. This in turn involves *courage* and *fortitude* – being able to 'hang in' when the going gets tough. *Prudence* and *practical wisdom* or discernment

---

1. See chapters 7 and 8 for an extended account of the calls of Abraham, Moses, Esther and Judith.

are also virtues which are underpinned and supported by the experience of having a call.

Vulnerability, Authenticity, and Transparency

A quite different set of personal spiritual experiences are feelings of being vulnerable and fragile, or of being insecure and fearful of being rejected. Closely linked to these, for some people, is the sense of being unworthy or not good enough, not deserving of respect. For other people the focus is rather more inward: there is a sense of being isolated and lonely.

Most of these feelings are ones which all of us experience at least occasionally and in some degree. For some people they are so deep and long-lasting that they are central components in their character. It is important to acknowledge such feelings, to allow them to surface in our awareness. For if we try to push them aside we are giving them more energy. Of course it is not healthy to allow ourselves to wallow in these negative feelings. But, properly handled, they can be deeply spiritual experiences.

The reality is that vulnerability and a certain degree of loneliness are a fundamental part of the human condition. It is important to recognise that, not merely in a notional way but at the heart level. If we do so, it gives a quality of depth and authenticity to our character which is deeply human and very attractive to others.

Properly handled, these experiences are an invitation to us to adopt and live by the moral values of authenticity, truth, and transparency. It is not just a matter of being truthful at the intellectual level, but of being in touch with our feelings, knowing what is going on within us. We are committed to developing an alignment within ourselves, so that our feelings are, by and large, in line with our moral commitments – with the way we want to be.

When I refer to the moral value of transparency I have in mind the way our authenticity comes across to others. When we speak to them they know at once that we mean what we say. They can feel the truth in us. This happens because our emotions are, by and large, in harmony with our reason and moral commitments. The result is that our words are backed up by the myriad of barely conscious non-verbal signals that always flow between people as they speak to each other.

This is an important aspect of a genuine spirituality. It is almost the exact opposite of the kind of puritan attitudes which many of us were brought up with. The practical assumption in a puritan spirituality is that virtue is bound to be difficult and painful – that it is a matter of going against our spontaneous feelings. Its motto might be taken to be 'the more pain the more gain'. A truly human and Christian spirituality, by contrast, has as a working assumption the view of St Thomas Aquinas that virtue is most truly itself when it comes easily to us. Of course it may not always feel that way, but it is the ideal towards which we are moving.

Identity and Rootedness

There is another spiritual experience which has to do with how individuals relate to themselves. It is a feeling of rootedness, of knowing one's identity, where one stands – and also what one stands for. There is an element of security in it, which balances but does not eliminate the element of insecurity which I noted previously.

For many people it is useful, perhaps even necessary, to engage in what is called assertiveness work. Through this they can learn to articulate clearly – and at times quite forcefully – what they believe in, what they stand for, and what they want. As they go on, they will no longer experience all this as hard work. It will become easy and natural, a part of what they are and an enjoyable way in which they nourish their spirituality. In this way the moral values and virtues of authenticity, clarity and truthfulness are underpinned and fostered by the experiences of identity and rootedness.

Primal people – that is, those living in traditional societies where there is little modern technological development – are generally well rooted. They live in traditional societies where their sense of identity is bound up with an experience of being part of an on-going continuity of life. They feel in touch with the ancestors from whom they have sprung. And the present generation expect to have children and descendents and, when their time comes, to move on and become part of the ancestral community.

People in modern technologically developed societies may find it useful to get in touch with their roots by researching the family tree and learning about those who have gone before them and on whose shoulders they now live. Perhaps even more important is to make a closer connection with nature – with the animal and plant world.

Beauty, Wonder, Oneness

Once again I quote some lines by Patrick Kavanagh, this time from his poem 'Canal Bank Walk':

> O unworn world enrapture me, encapture me in a web
> Of fabulous grass and eternal voices by a beech,
> Feed the gaping need of my senses, give me *ad lib*
> To pray unselfconsciously with overflowing speech
> For this soul needs to be honoured with a new dress woven
> From green and blue things and arguments that cannot be
> proven.[2]

Better than any words of mine, the poem gives a sense of what a deep spiritual experience it can be to come in touch with the beauty of nature. Earlier in the same poem, Kavanagh speaks of how the waters and banks of the canal are 'pouring redemption' for him. Many people have a similar experience, though they may not have expressed it in such powerfully poetic words as Kavanagh.

Those who live in a rural setting may take for granted the nourishment of spirit that comes from contact with nature and the distinct beauty that comes with each of the seasons. People who live in cities have to make more deliberate efforts to ensure that they make regular contact with the unspoiled parts of nature lest their spirits become drained, dried out, and impoverished.

Some time ago, I was in the Saõ Paulo area of Brazil, an urban sprawl of up to twenty million people with few green or open spaces. The friends with whom I was staying had just been given a young dog. This dog had been born in a crowded urban neighbourhood where he had never seen grass. I tried to entice him to walk on the little patch of lawn in front of his new home. But he refused to do so because this area of green grass was strange alien territory for him. For me this became a symbol of the world in which children there were growing up – a 'concrete jungle' which offered little to nourish the soul.

Primal people live 'close to the earth'. They experience themselves as an integral part of the web of life, directly in touch with the animal and plant life all around them. It is only to be expected,

2. *The Complete Poems*, Goldsmith Press, Newbridge, 1988, p 294.

then, that they feel themselves 'grounded' without ever having to think about it or work at it.

For us, however, it is not so simple. Many of us find ourselves floating in isolation, no longer in touch with some solid 'ground'. To overcome that sense of unconnectedness calls for a conscious and deliberate effort. We need to re-establish our links with nature and to cultivate these links. We may find it helpful to take time out to walk in the hills or to spend time in a wilderness location. Those who allow themselves to unwind, relax and exercise themselves in nature find it brings them peace of soul. In this way, the virtues of tranquillity, serenity, and groundedness are nourished and strengthened by the spiritual experience of being closely in touch with nature.

There are times in all of our lives when our contemplation of the beauty or majesty and power of nature evokes in us a deep sense of wonder. We find ourselves lifted out of ourselves in some degree and transported into a timeless realm. For some people this wonder is so all-consuming that they are taken up into what may be called an experience of nature-mysticism. Of course this state may only last for a short time. But when they return to the everyday world they often find that the quality of their lives has been greatly enriched.

The experience of the wonder and beauty of nature provides a solid basis for the value and virtue of ecological respect and sensitivity. There are many people who feel an obligation to safeguard the environment; but they find it a burdensome task because they are motivated solely by a sense of duty or guilt. But this burden can be transformed into a pleasure if they take time to savour the beauty and majesty of the natural world. I shall return to this topic in a later chapter.

An Answer to Prayer

There is one further spiritual experience which I wish to mention. It arises when one has come before God either in freedom of spirit or in desperation and made some specific request. This prayer may be just a wordless cry from the heart of somebody who turns in desperation to the God in whom he or she has apparently ceased to believe. On the other hand, it may be a deliberate plea addressed to a God with whom one has a deep personal on-going relationship. In either case, the spiritual experience I have in mind is the remarkable surge of gratitude and joy – mixed in, perhaps, with a tinge of surprise – which fills one's heart when one finds that this prayer has been answered.

This experience, too, provides a firm basis for a moral value. The value in this case is that of *dependency*. At a time when we place so much emphasis on independence it may seem odd to suggest that dependency is a genuine value. However, the dependency that is at issue here is not at all opposed to an authentic personal autonomy. What it brings home to us is that it is an illusion to imagine we can be fully independent.

The reality is that all of us live our lives from moment to moment with threats and dangers all around us: we may get a heart attack, or be struck by lightning, or lose the person that is dearest to us, or find ourselves crippled or unable to communicate with others. No insurance policy can cover us for the most frightening things that can happen to us quite 'out of the blue'. Furthermore, despite all our efforts to live independently, we rely on others for some of the most important aspects of our lives – for love and companionship, for a sense of community and teamwork, for security and peace where we live, and for the joy of receiving or giving gifts.

The shape of our lives is determined in fact by the conjunction of billions of different events happening all around us and over which we have little or no control. The sceptic may say we are the victims of chance. The believer may look at the same reality and say we are in the hands of Providence. But, however we interpret the pattern, it is only by closing our eyes to the truth that we can refuse to acknowledge our dependency. The only issue then is whether we choose to interpret it negatively as an unavoidable limitation or positively as a value. If we opt to see it as a value it can help us to avoid arrogance, overweening pride and selfishness. It can bring into our character a certain gentle humility and an openness and generosity towards others. Ultimately this value of dependency may lead us into a willingness to accept what life has to offer, and a trust in providence which is not fatalistic but is an acceptance of the small but nevertheless infinitely important part we are called to play in the co-creation of ourselves and our world.

CHAPTER THREE

Experience of Mystery

Those who take time to explore the various experiences I have been describing may find that from behind them all there emerges gradually a further and much deeper experience. It is a sense of the mystery which surrounds our lives. The very fact that it is mysterious means that it cannot be described in intellectual terms. But one can become aware of it in an obscure way through a range of feelings and sensations. Sometimes these come mixed up together. At other times we may find ourselves swinging slowly or rapidly from a sense of dryness and emptiness to a sense of wordless fullness; or moving from feelings of loss and regret to a sense of joy in the present and hope for the future; or from a sense of generalised remorse to an overwhelming awareness of being loved and forgiven.

I venture to suggest that this mystery may come into one's awareness in any one of four different modes. There are times when a person has what may be called 'a winter experience' or 'a desert experience' of the mystery. In this mode of the mystery there is little joy and few signs of life. Nevertheless, it may evoke a commitment to 'hang on' or 'hang in there'. This is perhaps the kind of nameless faith which is alluded to in the final words of the Bette Midler song 'The Rose':

> Just remember in the Winter,
> far beneath the bitter snows
> lies the seed that with sun's love
> in the Spring becomes the rose.

At other times the mystery may be experienced in a quite different mode. This time it brings with it a sense of new life beginning to spring up. So it might be described as 'a spring-time experience'. One may not yet be filled with joy, but there is an emerging sense that the hanging on was worthwhile. There is a freshness, a sense of new energy and new beginnings, of life re-asserting its victory over darkness or drought. Lots of exciting new possibilities are emerging. If the winter experience of the mystery offers a basis for the virtue of faith, this spring-time experience provides an underpinning for the virtue of hope.

There is a third mode in which one may experience the fundamental mystery which surrounds our lives. It may perhaps be called a 'flowering' mode of the mystery, analogous to our experience of summer. When we find ourselves in this mode, or this mood, there is a sense of hope fulfilled, of things coming together in a wondrously creative way. Life seems rich and colourful, and not merely meaningful but also benign. One is likely to experience short periods of pure joy. This 'flowering' experience of the mystery provides one with a rich underpinning for commitment to the value and virtue of love in its more active aspect.

Finally, we may find ourselves in touch with mystery in what might be called 'a harvest experience'. This is a time when one's life seems to have borne fruit. One may have a sense of achievement, of fulfilment. One may feel that this is the time to sit back and enjoy the fruits which have emerged from the efforts of the past.

However, in this harvest experience the focus is not mainly on one's efforts of the past. There is rather a feeling of being gifted. One has at times a sense of being immersed in the benevolence of nature, of friends and community, of life itself, and, perhaps, of God – or whatever ultimate power one senses behind it all. This 'harvest experience' of mystery offers one a solid foundation for the virtue of love – not so much this time in its active mode but in its more contemplative aspect.

Religions

The various religions of our world may be seen as attempts to symbolise and even to name – however inadequately – the mystery which surrounds our lives. We have much to learn from these different religions.

The primal religions of those who live in traditional societies help us to appreciate the spiritual dimensions of the web of life in which we all live. They help us to realise that the ultimate mystery is not a remote God but is present and at work in the world around us.

There is value in the near agnosticism of Buddhism, since it reminds us that ultimately the mystery cannot be named. But perhaps equally valuable is the way the Hindus so exuberantly name a multitude of deities, each of which gives expression to some aspect of the mystery. This is balanced by the severe emphasis in Islam and in orthodox Judaism on the transcendence or otherness of God.

Finally, in Christianity at its best we may find a carefully nuanced emphasis on all these elements. We acknowledge the God who is always beyond our understanding, but whom, with Jesus, we can call Abba. We see in Jesus this God made visible in our world, sharing our journey. And we open ourselves to the promptings of the mysterious Spirit who moves creatively within our world and within our hearts. Christians will, of course, find this briefest of summaries quite inadequate. So, since I am writing this book primarily for Christian believers, I shall devote the next three chapters to spelling out in a little more detail how committed Christians might understand the mystery which surrounds our lives.

Two Dimensions of Spirituality

As I pointed out in the Introduction, the word 'spirituality' has come to have two quite different shades of meaning. A lot of people understand it to refer to meditative practices or other ways of developing inward peace and mindfulness. Others tend to look outwards. In their view and their practice spirituality is mainly concerned with the major moral and political issues of our world. Care for the earth, interracial harmony, human rights, justice in the relationships between 'the North' and 'the South', play a central role in their spirituality. Indeed some of them may even be reluctant to use the word 'spirituality' since they associate it with undue preoccupation with the self. So they may prefer to speak of 'ethical commitment' instead of spirituality.

My hope is that what I have written here about spiritual experiences, moral values, and mystery, will go some way towards enabling readers to realise that both senses of the word 'spirituality' are valid – and also that each of them is essential if we are to develop a rich and rounded spirituality. For all of us it is important to maintain a certain balance between the contemplative and the active. It may be that at times they seem to pull us in opposite directions – outward to the world or inward towards our deepest self. But more fundamentally each of the two aspects needs the other. We may find it beneficial occasionally to switch for a time from having a primary focus on one to putting more emphasis on the other.

We must, however, acknowledge that any particular person is entitled to choose a way of life which gives more emphasis to one or the other of these two aspects. Some people are naturally activist, others are contemplative by nature. Furthermore, as we go through life each of us may make a major shift in which we move from one lifestyle to the other. Those who have been very outward-looking may feel the need to take 'time out' to go deep within themselves and then return renewed to the active life.

In general, we expect younger people to be quite active and older people to become rather more contemplative. But not everybody fits that pattern. What is important is that we do not adopt a readymade, *a priori* or ideological view of how our spiritual journey should go. Each of us needs to discover and explore his or her own call and to 'read the signs of the times' as they apply to each one of us personally. And we are all called to support each other on our different journeys and to celebrate the diversity of our calls as well as our common commitment.

CHAPTER FOUR

A Christian Approach to the Mystery

Perhaps the most important thing to be said about a Christian approach to the mystery that surrounds our life is that it does not remove the mystery. It throws light on the mystery we call God, it enriches our response to it, but it does enable us to fully understand God or eliminate the sense that we are in the presence of a reality that is beyond our reach. For this we must be very grateful because, if the mystery were absent, our lives would be impoverished and we would be left with something far less than the true God.

Benvolent, Personal, and Moral
Our Christian faith invites us to say and believe a number of important things about the mystery. First of all, we believe that the mystery within which we live is ultimately *benevolent*. I am using the phrase 'ultimately benevolent' here in two slightly different senses: in the sense that we cannot conceive of anything more benevolent than God; and in the sense that, though there are times when we find it difficult or even impossible to experience this benevolence, our belief is that in the long run the benevolent love of God will shine forth.

A second crucial aspect of our Christian faith is that God is *personal*. Of course God is not personal in just the same way as we humans are. From the point of view of spirituality, however, the important thing is that we believe we can speak to God, either in spoken words or in our hearts and minds, and that God hears what we have to say.

Thirdly, Christians believe that God is *moral*. This means that God never does anything that is evil and never demands that we take any action that is evil. Furthermore, it means that what makes an action good or evil is not simply some arbitrary decree of God. Rather it is whether or not it respects the order of nature.

Through observation and scientific study we can come to understand the order of the world – learning what kind of actions on our part damage the pattern of nature and what actions respect it and promote genuine development. God has given us the gift of intelligence which enables us to understand the pattern. Moreover, God gives each of us a conscience, an awareness of values and an invitation to respond to them. God respects our conscience.

Free

Furthermore, Christians insist that God is *free*. At first sight this may seem so obvious that it hardly needs to be said. But, the sad fact is that quite frequently religion becomes tainted or distorted by magical or superstitious ideas. The difference between true religion and magic is that those who practice magic are trying to 'harness' supernatural powers. Their aim is to control, or compel, or manipulate God – or a lesser quasi-divine agency – by engaging in some ritual practice.

A less extreme form of the same aberration is the superstitious belief that God has made a bargain with us. For instance, some people maintain that anybody who wears a certain scapular, or that one who says a certain prayer every day, or passes on a particular 'chain prayer', or 'does the nine First Fridays' will never go to hell, or is guaranteed to obtain some particular benefit. To imagine that God makes bargains of this kind is to think that we can earn some favour from God. This means that we are putting a limit to God's freedom.

What God has done instead is to invite us into a quite different kind of two-way relationship, which in the bible is called a covenant.

> I shall give you a new heart and a new spirit, taking out of your body your heart of stone and giving you a heart of flesh. I shall give you a new spirit so you shall keep my laws and discern and do my will. I will be your God and you shall be my people. (Ezekiel 36:26-8)

This is something far richer than a bargain: it involves a free two-way commitment based on a mutual promise. There is a crucial difference between this covenant and a bargain. If one party to a bargain fails to carry out what has been promised, then the whole bargain lapses. But, in the covenant, God remains faithful to the promise when we fail to live up to our side of the commitment – and even if we entirely renounce our promise.

God, being free, wants each one of us to be free. There are various aspects to our freedom. Leaving over to a later chapter a discussion of the political and economic aspects of liberation and freedom, I want here to focus on personal freedom of spirit in our relationship with God. I have learned from my own experience and that of others that if we are free in making our prayers we are much more likely to get a positive response from God.

It is helpful to start with the statement of Jesus in the gospel: 'Ask, and it will be given you; seek, and you will find; knock, and it will be opened to you. For every one who asks receives, and the one who seeks finds, and to the one who knocks it will be opened' (Lk 11:9-10). We are being invited to put our requests before God in a simple, direct, even childlike manner.

But is it true that such prayers will be answered as the words of the gospel suggest? In my experience it is true – provided we come before God in genuine freedom of spirit. This means that we have an inner freedom in making the prayer, because we are leaving God free to say 'yes', or 'no', or 'try again', or 'perhaps later'.

That is the kind of prayer that God seems to answer positively. Fundamentally, we are saying to God: 'I think it would be good if you were to grant my request, but I know that you know what is best for me so I trust you entirely.' However, this description seems to empty our prayer of its urgency and to suggest that we don't really care whether or not our prayer is answered. So we need to balance this by recalling the emphasis of Jesus on being persistent and even demanding in prayer (e.g. Lk 11:5-8 and Lk 18:1-5). This means that our prayers of petition should have an interesting combination of two qualities which at first sight may seem opposed to each other – an insistent urgency and a total trusting freedom of spirit.

Why should it be that one who prays in freedom of spirit is more likely to have the prayer answered? In terms of human psychology we might see it as rather similar to what happens when we fail to remember something no matter how hard we try; and then, when we stop trying, it pops into our mind. In much the same way, there are times when we are over-anxious to get what we are praying for. Then our prayer is coming from a neurotic or unfree part of us. In that case, God is slow to grant our request because God wants to lead us away from that kind of compulsiveness. On the other hand, once we have attained a measure of spiritual freedom we are far more likely to get a positive response from God. In this way God is 'training' us to work towards full spiritual freedom.

It is, of course, obvious that making any prayer of petition is a act of faith and trust. Perhaps less obvious is the fact that deciding that our prayer has been answered is also an act of faith, of trust in God. We make a request with a particular outcome in mind. But, quite frequently, our view on what constitutes a positive response will have changed by the time we decide that our prayer has been answered. This means that the 'success' of our prayers of petition cannot be measured statistically in strictly scientific terms.

Those who would like a proof that prayer 'works' may feel that what I have written in the previous paragraph is an evasion of the issue – a 'cop out'. But making a request of God is more like asking a favour of a friend than like putting money in a machine to buy a soft drink. Success or failure is easily measured when we put money in the slot. But our request of a favour from a friend is just the start of a dialogue with somebody whom we trust. The dialogue may lead us to see that our need can be met in a different way. So we may come to feel that our friend has responded positively to our request even though the response is different from what we had requested in the first place. In fact we may feel that what we have received is even better than what we had asked for. If this is true in the case of a request to a human friend, it is even more applicable to the prayers we ask God to answer. For God is not a slot-machine but an exceptionally trustworthy friend!

Presence of God
Central to the Christian faith is the conviction that the mystery

we call God is not remote 'at a distance' but is always fully present to our world and to each one of us. We do not have to escape out of the world in order to be in God's presence. Furthermore, we have the opportunity to make this a two-way relationship: God invites each of us to make ourselves fully present to this benevolent mystery. It is our privilege to come, as we have traditionally said, 'into the presence of God'.

Being present to God and allowing God to be present to us involves staying as far as possible in the present moment. Furthermore, being present to God is a matter of becoming more deeply present to ourselves. At first sight that statement may seem to be a contradiction in terms. So we need to remind ourselves that becoming present to God is not like becoming present to another human person. God is within us as well as beyond us.

What is required is a particular way of being present to ourselves. It is not the kind of concentration where we are looking at what is happening within us in a detached and objective way. Instead, we allow ourselves to sink into that more fuzzy awareness we can have of ourselves in our subjectivity rather than as a clearly defined object. Then we let that awareness extend outward into the mystery that surrounds us. For some of us this mystery is experienced and named as our loving God. Others may not wish to name the mystery as God; they may simply experience themselves as part of a wider mysterious whole. In either case we allow the mystery to be present to, and part of, our consciousness – to such an extent that our personal identity becomes to some extent lost in the mystery.

Many people have discovered that when we are truly present to ourselves and to God we share very fully in God's creative power. So, we become effective – even powerful – in an effortless way. Without manipulating or pushing others we can have a major influence on the people around us and can bring change in the wider society. The powerful effect we have on others arises not so much from anything we say or do. Rather, it comes mainly from *what we are* – from the quality of our presence to them.

One way of understanding how the experience of presence makes us powerful is to see it as bringing us into harmony with what we may call 'the flow of life'. Movement comes easily when we flow with the current of life. Things fall into place. And this seems to apply not only to our own actions but even to those of the people we meet. We find ourselves experiencing many examples of what Carl Jung would call synchronicity or meaningful coincidence, where there is no obvious causal relationship between the two events.

Some people will remain dissatisfied with this account in terms of synchronicity. They may insist on looking for a more concrete causal explanation for how our presence can have such a powerful effect on others. They may perhaps find a partial explanation by concluding that the sense of harmony with life which is evident in the way we are present is an invitation to those around us to come more in touch with the pattern of life and their place in it. As a result, they too begin to find that life is not always a struggle but that things slip easily into place and they can flow with life.

Creator

Our awareness of God's presence evokes in us a contemplative response. But there is also a more active side to God's presence in the world and in each of us. Our faith assures us that the mystery we call God is a *creator* and *life-giver* – and this is expressed very vividly in the biblical story of the valley of the bones (Ezekiel 37: 4-10):

> 'Prophesy to these bones' ... So I prophesied as I was commanded; and as I prophesied, there was a noise, and behold, a rattling; and the bones came together, bone to its bone ... 'Prophesy to the breath' ... So I prophesied ... and the breath came into them, and they lived, and stood upon their feet, an exceedingly great host.

This story conveys very vividly the idea that our life is a share in the life-breath of God. But in our everyday life we cannot expect to see the divine life-giving power at work in such an obvious and overt manner. There is a mysterious quality to the way God works in the world and in us: the divine power nearly always seems to come 'in disguise'. A more traditional way of saying this is that God acts through what theologians call 'secondary causes'. This means that God does not have to intervene

40

directly in our world but acts through our free human actions and through the millions of events that take place in the natural world and through the whole process of evolution.

This is not the place to explore philosophically how there is room for God to be at work in the trillions of apparently chance events that make up the pattern of evolution. It suffices to say that we are no longer trapped in the mechanistic conception of the universe which would at most allow God to be outside the process like a great clockmaker. Consequently, very many scientists reject as outmoded the view of Richard Dawkins that science and religious faith are irrevocably opposed to each other. In fact there is a beautiful convergence of the two in what Thomas Berry calls 'The New Story of Creation' in which evolution plays a central role.[1] I shall return to this topic in Chapter 12 which is devoted to an ecological spirituality.

Providence, Co-Creation and Prayer
Belief in the providence of God follows from the conviction that God is utterly benevolent and is totally present to every aspect of our lives. Providence means that God cares about us and for us – and not in the rather futile way that we may at times care about some far-away disaster. God's care for each of us is specific, effective, on-going and intimate. The words of Jesus in the gospel are quite clear about this:

> Look at the birds of the air: they neither sow nor reap nor gather into barns, and yet your heavenly Father feeds them. Are you not of more value than they? … And why are you anxious about clothing? Consider the lilies of the field, how they grow; they neither toil nor spin; yet I tell you, not even Solomon in all his glory was arrayed like one of these. But if God so clothes the grass of the field, which today is alive and tomorrow is thrown into the oven, will God not much more clothe you, O people of little faith? (Mt 6:26-30)

An important aspect of our Christian faith is that God is not

1. Thomas Berry, *The Dream of the Earth*, San Francisco (Sierra Club Books: 1988), especially pp 123-137. See also Brian Swimme, *The Hidden Heart of the Cosmos: Humanity and the New Story*, Maryknoll (Orbis Books: 1996).

merely creator but co-creator. In other words, we humans are invited to be co-creators, partners with God in the process of shaping the world and in creating ourselves and our communities. God acts not merely through the process of evolution but also through our free human choices. This co-creation – a convergence of God's action and ours – is a key element in an authentically Christian spirituality.

It is relatively easy to believe that God is working through us when we care for the sick, or rear children, or even when we cultivate the soil and produce food. But we need to go a step further. Think of a parent, who having washed and fed a child, just sits watching and loving that child. Surely that contemplative love is also creative? Do we not at times even experience it as a positive creative energy which generates an aura of love in which the child can blossom? In this way the parent is sharing in the creative love of God for the child, even when he or she is not taking any obvious outward action.

A fully Christian spirituality invites us to take yet another step forward into the mystery of creativity. Think of a parent of a sick child who holds that child up in prayer to God. Earlier in this chapter, I suggested that such a prayer is more likely to be answered when it is made in freedom of spirit. Now I shall try to answer the question, how does this take place?

In the past, people tended to see the parent's prayer as a request that God 'intervene' in, and even disrupt, the natural process of the child's illness in order to heal the child. But an authentically modern Christian spirituality can look at this prayer in a different way – a way that respects the order of nature. God does not have to 'intervene' because God has been present in the process from the beginning. There is no need for God to 'break the rules' of nature because the laws of nature do not work in a deterministic way. The processes have a certain open-endedness to them. There is room for a coincidence of happenings at the chemical and biological levels that can bring healing to the child without any disruption of the laws of physics or chemistry or biology. Furthermore, the prayer of the parent may be seen as generating an energy which plays a key part in the healing. So the prayer is an act of co-creation, rather than just a request to God to intervene from outside the process.

Against the background of this approach to spirituality, it is helpful to return to a biblical language and speak of 'marvels' rather than of 'miracles'. In biblical times both words meant much the same thing. The root word in the term 'miracle' is simply something that evokes awe in us – a marvellous event.

The problem about miracles arose a few hundred years ago when Western scientists began to think in terms of rigid almost mechanical 'laws of nature'. In that context a miracle came to mean a direct intervention by God which disrupted the pattern by breaking the laws of nature. Now that we have moved on from such a mechanistic understanding of the processes of nature we can have a less rigid conception of miracles or marvels. This means that we can feel free to make our petitions confidently and frequently to God, without specifying whether we are asking for a miracle or just an 'ordinary' answer to prayer. Certainly we can at times pray that God's response will be the bringing about of something that is truly marvellous – a healing or other event that was so highly unlikely that it evokes in us awe and boundless gratitude.

In this chapter I have been exploring some key elements in the Christian approach to the mystery that surrounds our life and that we call God. There remains a great deal more to said on this topic so, in the next chapter, I shall move on to consider God's Spirit and God's Word. However, all through these chapters it is important to remember that all our efforts to describe God in words are quite inadequate. Our words, whether they be eloquent and comprehensive or just a half articulate cry from the heart, have to be balanced by a long silence in which we bow before the inexpressible mystery which Christians call God.

CHAPTER FIVE

God's Spirit and God's Word

God is spirit. This may seem so obvious that it hardly needs to be said. Nevertheless it has very important implications. It means, among other things, that we cannot pin God down in one place. More significantly, it means that we can make contact with God wherever we happen to be. There is a beautiful passage in St John's gospel where Jesus says: 'The hour is coming, and now is, when the true worshippers will worship the Father in spirit and truth ... God is spirit, and those who worship God must worship in spirit and in truth' (Jn 4:23-4). God is 'available' to us at any time, in any place, and in every possible situation. The only limits to our contact with God are those which we impose on ourselves.

Those who wrote the various books of the Old Testament did not make any distinction between 'God' and 'the Spirit of God'. It was only with the coming of Jesus there began a process of a rather gradual recognition of the Holy Spirit as in some sense distinct from the Word and from the One whom Jesus addressed as Abba. It took time before there was a clear affirmation that there are three persons in our one God.

If our Christian spirituality is to be authentic we need to realise that the word 'person' as we understand it at the present time was not at all what was meant by the word 'person' when the Creeds were formulated. Originally, the Latin word *persona* meant a mask; and even in English today we speak of a person putting on a particular 'persona', meaning a role that they play. That is quite different from what we now mean by the word 'person'. We take it for granted nowadays that what distinguishes one person from another is that each of them has the power to think for herself or himself and the power to make his or her own decisions. But part of our Christian faith is that this is not true of the Blessed Trinity: in God there is only one mind and one will.

In our everyday thinking, praying and conversation it might perhaps be better to see the three persons of the Trinity as three 'faces' of God. We could leave the word 'person' for more academic theology where it would be understood that it is a technical historically-conditioned term which has an important and specific meaning – but not the same meaning as the term has in everyday language today.

Many Christians seem to think of the Trinity as just an incomprehensible aspect of God which has no obvious relevance to spirituality and prayer. Others try to make the Trinity relevant to our spirituality by proposing the misleading idea that it is the perfect model for human community – as though the three persons had to have a dialogue with each other and work out a consensus of their different views. The advantage of thinking in terms of 'three faces of God' is that it could help to make the Trinity immediately relevant to the way we live out our spirituality.

A first 'face' of God is the benevolent, provident, and co-creative God described in the previous chapter. This is the God who, nevertheless, remains mysterious, beyond our comprehension; the prodigal God who beckons us onwards on our journey and awaits us at its end.

A second 'face' of God is the divine Spirit who has been hovering and moving over the waters of creation from the very beginning (cf Gen 1:2), breathing life and variety and bubbling creative energy into our universe, and guiding from within the whole process of evolution. This divine Spirit is also the one we see as inspiring the prophets of Old Testament times and also thousands of other inspired people – Christian and non-Christian – down through the ages.

Perhaps most important of all is the way we attribute to the Holy Spirit the presence of God in the lives in each of us, joining with our own spirit in declaring that we are God's children, and causing us to groan in expectation of a new creation (Rom 8:22-3). We experience this Spirit helping us in our weakness, praying in us, pleading with God on our behalf in sighs too deep for words (Rom 8:26). As Christians we believe that it is the Spirit who moves us to compassion for people in trouble, and brings those marvellous gifts which we call 'the fruits of the Spirit' –

love, joy, peace, patience, generosity, gentleness, faithfulness, and so on (Gal 5:22-3). These gifts are the expression of the love of God which, quite gratuitously, is poured out into our hearts (Rom 5:5).

This is a love which we should normally be able to experience as it warms the human heart. As we develop a greater sensitivity to the gentle touch of God's Spirit we find ourselves growing in an awareness of being loved and lovable, as well as in the inner freedom which enables us to respond in love. We are reminded that the Spirit is the living love of God. To describe this 'Spirit-face-of-God' we can borrow a phrase from St John of the Cross: 'the Living Flame of Love'.

We also associate the Spirit with our sense of being guided, giving us a 'feel' for what God would like us to do at any given moment. When we feel swamped by a multitude of options, or when we feel trapped with little or no choice, we can turn to the Spirit and ask for guidance. Within the Christian tradition there is a rich resource of reflection and wisdom on how best to get in touch with the movements of the Spirit as we try to discern where God is leading us.[1]

The Holy Spirit is at work in our hearts and is nearer to us than we are to ourselves. But there remains a mysterious quality to the presence and action of the Spirit. We call to mind the words which St John's gospel puts in the mouth of Jesus: 'Just as you can hear the wind but can't tell where it comes from or where it will go next, so it is with the Spirit' (Jn 3:8 *Living Bible* version). This passage reminds us of what we might call the anonymous work of the Spirit 'behind the scenes' in people all over the world, including millions of ordinary people who may never have named, or even heard of, the Holy Spirit.

---

1. I have written extensively on this topic of discernment in the final three chapters and the appendix of my book *Spirituality of Leadership* (Dublin, Columba Press, 2006; US title *Faith at Work*, Liturgical Press, Collegeville, 2007). I suggested there that if we wish to discern well it is important that we be 'affectively converted'. What this means is that we are in touch with our feelings – and that our feelings are, by and large, in line with our fundamental commitments.

The Word of God

I have noted already that Christians believe that God is personal and that we can speak to God. But does God speak back to us? Is there real dialogue with God? Christians have to give a nuanced answer to this question. Only very few people have a sense that God is communicating directly with them by dropping words directly into their mind or through letting them hear a spoken voice from God. But part of Christian belief is that God communicates with us in other ways: through the beauty and wonder of creation, as well as through the various ways God 'answers' our prayers. Many of us go further: we believe that God is 'speaking' to us through the events of our everyday lives – for instance, through our meeting up with people who make an impact on us and through fortuitous coincidences that touch us deeply.

Down through the ages, people of many different cultures and religions look for something more – for some clear message in words from God. In Old Testament times the Jewish people believed that God spoke directly to the prophets and through them spoke to the people. When the words of the prophet were passed on to later generations, these were still seen as the explicit word of God; and when they were written down they became the scriptures. As Christians we continue to see these scriptures as the word of God. And we are assured that this word can have a powerful influence in our lives and on our world:

> As the rain and the snow come down from the sky
> and do not return before having watered the earth,
> fertilising it and making it germinate
> to provide seed for the sower and food to eat,
> so it is with the word that goes from my mouth:
> it will not return to me unfulfilled
> or before having carried out my good pleasure
> and having achieved what it was sent to do.
> (Is 55:10-11)

Jesus as Word of God

The unique and extraordinary aspect of the Christian approach to the mystery is a conviction that God is not content to communicate with us through signs and through the words of the

prophets. We believe that the divine love longs for a more intimate relationship with us. God wants to share the joys, worries,
uncertainties, disappointments, sufferings, and even the death
that is part of what it means to be human. That is why Jesus
came to live among us, as a third 'face' of God. It means that as
Christians we now see what we may call 'the human face' of
God, that is, God as willing to be friends with us in a fully
human way – and therefore prepared to be vulnerable, to be
scapegoated, and even to be murdered.

In his letter to the Colossians, Paul says: 'Jesus is the image of
the invisible God … for in him all the fullness of God was
pleased to dwell' (Col 1:15, 19). The Preface for the feast of
Christmas spells this out more fully in this beautiful description
of the role of Jesus: '… in him we see our God made visible, and
so we are caught up in the love of the God we cannot see.' This
brings out the fact that the purpose of God becoming present in
Jesus is to make the divine love so evident to us that we are
drawn into that love and invited to respond in love.

We call Jesus the Word of God because God speaks to us so
clearly through the words, the actions, and the life and death of
Jesus. We can even say that in Jesus the mystery is revealed (cf
Eph 1:9; 3:2-6; Col 1:26-7; 4:3). But of course we must remember
that to reveal a mystery is not at all like solving a puzzle. When
somebody solves a puzzle it is no longer a puzzle to that person.
But what happens when the mystery of the saving love of God is
revealed in Jesus? It simply means that the mystery is no longer
just the horizon against which we live out our lives but is now
also present in human history in the person of Jesus.

This Jesus who unveils for us the otherwise incredible love of
God, is himself an inexhaustible mystery. Down through the
ages, millions of saintly people have devoted their whole lives to
plumbing the mystery that is Jesus – meditating on his words,
contemplating his life and death, modelling their lives on his. By
doing so they have left us a boundless treasure of insights and
wisdom. Nevertheless they themselves assure us that he remains a limitless mystery which they feel they have barely
touched. In Chapter 9 below I hope to explore this mystery further by examining the call of Jesus.

Mystery

Before moving on from the reflections on God in these two chapters, I note again the title of the previous chapter, namely, 'A Christian Approach to the Mystery'. It seems better to use the word 'approach' rather than 'understanding' or 'interpretation', because Christians do not claim to have understood God. The work of the Spirit and the coming of Jesus throw great light on the mystery that is God. But they also add new depth to this mystery.

We are invited and challenged, as individuals and in our communities, to continue to explore, begging the Spirit to give us an ever deeper insight into the words of Jesus and of the scripture, as well into our Christian tradition. We also look outward to the wider world for further light on the mystery, aware that the Spirit continues to work in non-Christian religions and in the hearts of people everywhere.

Having acknowledged that our Christian account of God remains incomplete and inadequate, we must face the question whether it is valid and true as far as it goes. Once again, a nuanced answer is called for. As Christians we do not claim that what we believe about God and Jesus can be proved by purely rational arguments. We do, however, maintain that our belief is not irrational. By faith we go beyond reason—though not against it.

I find it helpful to see our human contribution to faith as a leap of hope. I hope that the mystery which surrounds our lives is the kind of God described in these two chapters, because otherwise I would find my life empty and pointless. I cannot justify this hope in a purely theoretical way. But I am prepared to make my leap of hope by acting as if this interpretation of the mystery is a valid one. So I freely choose to commit my life to the belief that it is true. The response of God is the gift of faith – a sense that my commitment is worthwhile and that as I live an authentic spirituality day by day I can experience the validity and rightness of my choice.

CHAPTER SIX

'Reading the Signs of the Times'

The phrase 'the signs of the times' is attributed to Jesus in the gospels (Mt 16:3). It is a term which has come to be used quite a lot by Christians within the past generation. The phrase generally refers to some public current happening which calls our attention to a significant change that is taking place in the world. When we speak of 'the signs of the times' we are not normally referring to happenings that are seen by only a relatively small number of people. The phrase refers rather to important political, social, or economic events or developments which are widely known – but whose full significance may not be widely understood.

It is usually assumed that the deeper meaning of the event or trend can be grasped only by those who 'read the signs' in the light of faith. In fact, as Christians understand it, the reading of the 'signs of the times' is an activity that requires a high degree of faith.

The reason why people are invited to read 'the signs of the times' is in order to help them to make a good discernment about how they ought to act. It is of course obvious that any such discernment has to take account of the various moral values and virtues which I noted in the first two chapters of this book. However, even full acceptance of all of these values and virtues only provides us with a general framework for good behaviour. It does not tell us how we should act in any particular situation. That is why we need to make a personal discernment in each specific case. In this context many Christians have come to believe that key events or trends are used by God as signs to enable us to understand something of the deeper meaning of what is taking place in the world. We can then make our discernment in the light of this deeper understanding.

Signs

The key point in all this is that these events or trends in the world are *signs*. A sign is something more than an event. It is a means of communication between intelligent beings. When we speak of 'the signs of the times' we are suggesting that God is sending us a message through these historical events. This means that, if we read the 'signs of the times' correctly, we are being enabled by God to *interpret* more accurately what is really going on in the world, behind the superficial appearances. Having come to understand something of the deeper significance of the situation we are then in a position make our decision and to *respond* to what is going on.

A sign is a communication between people. This means that the 'signs of the times' are more than merely *objective* historical events. They also have a personal *subjective* aspect. Here we are dealing with communication between God's Spirit and us humans who wish to read these signs. The 'message' is always an inter-personal one which involves not just objective data but also a strong emotional element. As the moral theologian Kevin Kelly says, it involves 'intelligently listening to the deepest hopes and desires, sufferings and anxieties, of the human family of today.'[1]

This means that one aspect of the signs is the emotional responses and reactions of people to the events and trends in the world. And we are not just observing these reactions but resonating with them. Kelly is suggesting that it is not a matter of noting the events and responses in a coldly intellectual manner; rather we are allowing ourselves to be profoundly moved by the deep feelings of people as they react to what is happening. Consequently, it is not helpful to make too sharp a distinction between the signs as objective events and our subjective reading of the signs.

The central point here is that the way the 'message' is heard by us is by allowing it to touch our hearts. So, in reading 'the signs of the times', we look first of all at our own *feeling* response to what is going on in the world and the reactions of people to these events. This is well put by Kevin Kelly who says, 'the signs of the times have to be *felt*'. He goes on to speak of how 'the

1. Kevin T. Kelly, *New Directions in Moral Theology: The Challenge of Being Human*, London: Chapman, 1992, p 22.

human spirit, moved by God's own Spirit, recoils in horror from whatever is dehumanising and violating respect for persons in our world today'. Our reaction to what is happening around us is an emotional one, coming in the form of 'anger, repugnance, horror, fear, anxiety, as well as the positive emotions of hope, expectation, determination, courage, etc.'[2]

The implication here is that the Holy Spirit is evoking in us a reaction to what is happening – one that is similar in some degree to God's own reaction. When we see and feel people being oppressed or degraded, we share the anger and sadness of God at this violation of human dignity. When we find the earth being polluted and exploited, once again our reaction of outrage mirrors that of God. On the other hand, when we see people being treated respectfully and observe genuine human development taking place, our joyful reaction is in some sense a share in the delight of God that the world and its people are living and acting in justice and love as God wants us to live.

Not a Code

Down through the ages – and perhaps particularly in more recent times – there have been some very misguided ideas about signs sent by God. There are Gnostic groups who believe that they have a secret wisdom which enables them to read signs from God which only they can understand. Some Christian sects or groups believe that the Book of the Apocalypse (Book of Revelation) contains various prophetic signs referring mainly to the end of the world. This is a superstitious and almost magical approach, one which treats signs from God as though they could be deciphered in the way one would decipher a message sent in code.

A code is an arbitrary extrinsic meaning added on to the normal or intrinsic meaning of something. For instance, in 1775, during the American war of independence Paul Revere arranged a coded signal with the sexton of a local church: one lantern in the steeple would be a sign that the British army were travelling by a land route; on the other hand, two lanterns would signal that they had chosen to travel by water across the Charles River.

---

2. 'Confessions of an Aging Moral Theologian' *The Furrow* Vol 25 (February 2004), p 89.

A genuine Christian 'reading' of the signs is something quite different from interpreting a code. It is not a matter of discovering a meaning added on from outside to something that is happening in the world. It is rather the discernment of a fuller or deeper meaning of an event or trend. It gives us some sense of how it fits into the unfolding of God's plan, which for the Christian is the coming of the Reign of God. It enables us to have at least a *glimpse* of the way that God sees what is taking place in the world.

I emphasise the word 'glimpse' which I used in the previous sentence. For, despite all our efforts to read 'the signs of the times', we still see things only 'through a foggy mirror' (1 Cor 13:12). Nevertheless, even this dim and tentative sense of God's viewpoint gives us some guidance in our discernment. It puts us in a somewhat better position to know how we should respond and how we should play our part in advancing the coming of the Reign of God.

Which Events are Signs?

How are we to know which events are 'signs of the times'? I think the best way to answer this question is to accept that, if we are sensitive to the movements of the Spirit and in harmony with the mind of Jesus, then any event can be seen as such a sign. However, some remarkable happenings are rather obvious 'signs of the times' – so they can be recognised even if we are somewhat slow in heart like the disciples at Emmaus (Lk 24:25).

Some of these signs are encouraging while others are alarming and may be seen as warnings from God. The fall of the Berlin wall in 1989 and the inauguration of Nelson Mandela as president of a free multi-racial South Africa in 1994 would count as encouraging signs. For people in Ireland and Britain – and indeed for many others—the signing of the Good Friday peace agreement in Northern Ireland in 1998 was a very positive sign of the times. Among the more alarming signs are the '9/11' attack on the Twin Towers in New York in 2001, hurricane Katrina which devastated New Orleans in 2005, and the recent very rapid melting of the Greenland ice-cap.

Under the guidance of the Holy Spirit we can interpret even the very frightening 'signs of the times' in the context of our

Christian hope. We believe that God's plan for us and for our world is a benevolent one and that 'God can write straight with crooked lines'. The challenge for us is to see what positive good is to be drawn out of events which at first sight seem utterly negative. For example, we may perhaps see the melting of the Arctic ice-cap as a wake-up call to us to change our environmentally damaging lifestyle. And we may see '9/11' as a warning that the peoples of 'the West' need to take urgent action to remedy the plight of the Palestinian people and, more generally, of the poor of the world. Perhaps also we should interpret is as an indication that we in the West should engage in serious political and religious dialogue with Muslim countries and peoples.

Tentative

I have used the word 'perhaps' twice in the previous paragraph. This is an indication that there has to be a tentative quality to the way we interpret 'signs of the times'. It is important to hold in our minds that, in all our attempts to read the signs, we are dealing with the mystery that Christians call God. And, as I have said, in anything to do with this mystery we can only see in a hazy way as in a foggy mirror (cf 1 Cor 13:12).

Furthermore, we have to allow for the fact that many of our judgements are made on the basis of unwarranted assumptions which we have failed to question. All of us are prejudiced in one way or another. Some of our prejudices are purely personal. Others are biases which are common to whole groups of people. For instance, very many upper and middle class people are prejudiced in assuming that they know better than the poor what is good for society. This is a point to which I shall return in Chapter 17 which deals with a spirituality of liberation.

Faith, not Divination

In all of this, there is one crucial point which I wish to emphasise: 'reading the signs of the times' is an act of faith, not of divination. What I mean by this may perhaps become clear by looking at two possible analogies from the secular world. The first of these is the way a water-diviner interprets the tremor in her hands as a sign that there is water under the ground. I want to say that this is not a good analogy for our reading of 'the signs of the times'.

A far more appropriate analogy can be found if we look at a situation where I am given a gift by another person. If the giver is somebody whom I do not trust, or whom I know does not like me, then I may suspect that the person is trying to bribe me. On the other hand, if the giver of the gift is a close friend, or is somebody in whom I have full trust, then I interpret the gift as a sign of the giver's love or gratitude or respect. The point is that in both cases I 'read' the meaning of the gift in the light of my prior relationship with the other.

In much the same way, our reading of 'the signs of the times' is done entirely in the light of our prior faith and trust in God. One may even say that we are reading a particular meaning into what is happening around us. We are assuming that God's hand is at work in the situation. We are also assuming that God is communicating with us through what is happening – and that the message is one which is designed to help us. But it depends mainly on ourselves whether we are inclined to interpret this help as encouragement or as a warning – or even, perhaps, as a punishment.

Does this understanding of our reading of 'the signs of the times' empty it of all real significance? Does it mean that the signs are so ambiguous and our reading so tentative that the whole process is of no real help in our discerning of how we ought to act? At first sight it may seem so. But perhaps we should think of the way relationships play out between people who are deeply in love with each other. Each of them is willing to devote endless hours to picking up clues which may throw light on how the other is feeling about particular issues or about the world in general. Do they see this as a pointless exercise, a waste of time? Not at all. They experience it as one of the many ways in which their love for each other is expressed and nourished. Similarly, our attempts to read the mind of God by examining 'the signs of the times' is a way in which we manifest and deepen our faith and give expression to our preoccupation with the things of God.

But can this help us in the process of discernment? Yes, it can – but not in the obvious way of giving us clear instructions about how to act. Rather it draws us more deeply into an exploration of the mind and heart of God. And, when we come to think of it, perhaps that is what God is most concerned about. As we are drawn more and more deeply into the love and the interests of God, we become increasingly sensitive to inspirations of the Spirit in regard to which of our possible actions are most in conformity with God's will for us and for the world. The result is that the most important element in our process of discernment is no longer our own attempt to read the signs; it is rather the movements of the Holy Spirit in our minds and hearts.

PART II

Personal Call:
In the Bible and in our own Lives

Here I am, Lord. Is it I, Lord?
I have heard you calling in the night.
I will go, Lord, if you lead me.
I will hold your people in my heart.
(Chorus of the hymn by Daniel L Schutte)

I don't know who—or what—put the question. I don't know when it was put. I don't even remember answering. But at some moment I did answer Yes to someone – or something – and from that hour I was certain that existence is meaningful and that, therefore, my life, in self-surrender, had a goal.
(Dag Hammarskjöld, *Markings*, p 169)

If a man [*sic*] does not keep pace with his companions, perhaps it is because he hears a different drummer. Let him step to the music he hears, however measured or far away.
(Henry David Thoreau).

CHAPTER SEVEN

The Call of Abraham and Our Call

In this second section of the book I invite readers to explore their own personal call by looking at the call of six characters from the bible – three men and three women. I begin with the story of Abraham, who is seen as 'the father of three faiths': Judaism, Christianity, and Islam.

We do not know whether or not Abraham was a single historical figure. The first written accounts of him come from hundreds of years after the time he was said to have lived. His story is a powerful myth which may be an account which is historically accurate. It may, on the other hand, be an amalgamation of the experiences of several different people or may even be a creation of the biblical authors. But, if it is not historically accurate, this makes the story all the more relevant because it means that those who told and wrote his story picked out and amalgamated or created those elements that are most significant for an understanding of what it means to get a personal call from God.

Abraham was called to leave his own land and his own people and to go forth in faith into a land which God promised to show him (Gen 12:1). Inextricably linked to this call was a promise by God that he would be blessed and would become the parent of many descendents. Later in the story we hear that Abraham had to wait for many years, and had his faith in God's promise sorely tested, before the promise was fulfilled.

In this account, Abraham's call and promise seems to come out of the blue; but another version of the story provides an interesting background to them. The Qur'an and other Islamic writings tell us that when Abraham (or Ibrahim as the Qur'an calls him) was a boy he destroyed the idols of his people, that is, the images of their gods. He was to be punished for this crime by being burned alive. But God rescued him from the fire. This part of the story suggests that from an early age Abraham was dissatisfied with the experience and understanding of the divine which had been given to him from his own culture. He was searching for a richer spiritual experience and was prepared to risk his life for this commitment.

We too

All this can enrich our own experience and understanding of our call. For many of us Christians, as for Abraham, our call is rooted in an experience of God which opens up an unexpectedly rich, exciting and challenging new possibility for us. Like Abraham we may find that the call involves leaving behind the place where we were 'at home', letting go of all that is familiar to us. The call is an invitation to step forward into the unknown and to face the prospect of surviving and thriving in it. We may be asked to go out in faith into a new and unknown situation – one which will gradually be unveiled for us by God.

In some cases the call may be evident to those around us. For instance, those who feel a call to enter a monastery or a convent, or to be a foreign missionary, have to leave home in a literal sense. But for many others the call may not be publicly visible. It may nevertheless involve a quite radical change of lifestyle. Perhaps it is a call to leave a comfortable job and take the risk of joining or establishing a programme of care for the earth or for the defence of human rights. It may be a call to devote oneself full-time to writing poetry or to painting or sculpture. For many people it is probably the call to give up a life of casual sexual relationships and to take the risk of following their heart and settling down with one partner.

The call comes 'from beyond'. For those who, like Abraham, experience such a radical call, there is probably a background experience which disposes them to hear God's call. It is a feeling of dissatisfaction with the existing order – a sense that there are idols in their world which cannot bring true human fulfilment. It is this disillusionment with the idols of their culture – wealth and power and 'success' – which leads them to take the risk of rejecting these false gods which are the powers of their world. Looking for a more authentic fulfilment they embark on a search for a spiritual experience which can fulfil the deepest longing of their heart.

As in the case of Abraham, their call is linked to a promise. For them, as for him, the promise is that their venturing forth into the unknown will not be in vain. In God's own time, their lives and work will eventually bear fruit. In the way the story of Abraham is told in the bible this promise is very clear and explicit; but we may suspect that in reality it was by no means so clear. However that may be in his case, we know, from our own experience, and that of others with whom we have been in contact, that the promise that one's deepest heart's desire will be fulfilled often seems no more than a vague hope. It can easily get almost buried under more immediate desires and pressures and disappointments. Indeed it seems like a miracle of grace that one can still cling on to that hope. Furthermore, we learn from the story of Abraham that those who experience a radical call like his, may have to endure a long period of waiting and trial – and apparent failure – before the promise is fulfilled.

One Fundamental Call
The bible tells us that God spoke to Abraham on several occasions and that he had to go through various stages on his journey. But it becomes clear that what he experienced was one fundamental call rather that a succession of different calls. This call unfolded gradually over his lifetime and stretched him more and more until it reached a climax in the call to sacrifice his son. Time after time he had to make decisions to follow the call and live in the hope generated by the promise. His basic decision had to be re-affirmed at times in very difficult circumstances.

There were times when following the call had painful and divisive consequences for Abraham. For instance, on his journey to the Promised Land he had to part from Lot his son-in-law and friend; and in doing so he had to let go the prospect of settling in a rich and fertile land, leaving it instead to Lot. Later on he was called to banish his partner Hagar and his first-born son Ishmael. And eventually he saw himself as being called to sacrifice the child who was dearest to him.

For people nowadays, too, the call is likely to be one fundamental reality which unfolds gradually over time. And they have to respond freely not just once for all but at each stage – and sometimes in difficult circumstances. Following the call may at times have painful and divisive consequences. There will be times when they have to uproot themselves, making painful decisions and letting go of relationships or possessions or comfortable surroundings. They may even find that, like Abraham, at some point the decision to continue to follow their call involves a willingness to relinquish something that seemed invaluable, or somebody that was dearest to them.

Dilemmas

It is interesting to note that Abraham found himself at various stages in a serious personal dilemma. On each of these occasions the dilemma arose when Abraham, while following his personal call, was confronted with the need or demand of 'the other'. By that I mean that following his call meant intersecting with and affecting other persons, each of whom had his or her own unique call and were each on their own unique journey. For instance, Abraham's commitment to following his call had major implications for the two women in his life – Sarah and Hagar.

In the bible, both of them come across mostly as rather meekly going along with the plans of Abraham as he seeks to follow his call while safeguarding his own interests. It is clear, however, that God does not accept Abraham's assumption that his personal call is so important that the welfare of others must always take second place. In Egypt, Abraham seeks to protect himself by persuading Sarah to pretend that she is his sister rather than his wife. However, when the ruler Abimelech takes Sarah into his harem, God intervenes to protect her from his attentions. Similarly, when Abraham has to banish Hagar and their child Ishmael, God tells him that God has great plans for this child (Gen 21:13). And, when Hager ran away on an earlier occasion, God's messenger intervened directly (Gen 16:10) to reveal to her that her son is destined to be the father of a great nation (the Arabs).

Obviously, Abraham's call to sacrifice his dearest child had a major impact on Isaac (in the Jewish version of the story) or on Ishmael (in the Islamic version). Abraham's dilemma was that it was apparently impossible for him to be true to his call (as he understood it at that moment) while also being respectful of 'the other', that is, taking full account of the need or welfare of the child he felt called to kill.

As Christians today we too find ourselves at times in a some-what similar dilemma – one that arises from the difficulty of being true to our call while also being fully respectful of 'the other'. There are obvious examples of this in the field of ecumenism and inter-religious dialogue. How can we be truly respectful of the vision and call of other Christians and people of other religions, while being faithful to our own call to share the good news of Jesus as understood by our own church? In the more personal sphere, each of us can think of situations where following our call may have created great difficulties for those around us.

The resolution of the dilemma, for us as for Abraham, comes about not through a rational linear process but through what we may call 'a revelatory moment', which brings about a breakthrough or transformation. In the story, this revelatory moment is presented as a miraculous intervention by God. For instance, when Abraham was a boy he was saved by God from being burned to death; and, much later in Egypt, when Abimelech wanted to marry Sarah or have her in his harem, God prevented him from touching her.

Of course the most serious of the dilemmas faced by Abraham arose when he felt called to sacrifice his son. The usual lesson which both Christian and Muslim scholars draw from this is that at times God may test our faith by demanding that we sacrifice that which is dearest to us. Very recently a mother told me how she found a profound truth in this traditional understanding of the story. She had waited for many years to have her first child and eventually her hope was fulfilled. Understandably, then, she focused all her love on this longed-for child. However, there came a time when she realised that she was in danger of allowing her love to drift into a kind of idolatry. She knew then that God was, in a sense, calling her to let go what was dearest to her. Of course this did not mean giving up her love for the child. Rather, it meant abandoning possessiveness and a kind of exclusivity in her love – something which would be damaging for both mother and child. She had to leave the child space to find its own direction in life and at the same time broaden the focus of her own love, so that she could also reach out to others.

For me, this was a profoundly moving story. It taught me that the customary interpretation of Abraham's sacrifice can be very significant for some people. However, I believe that it is better not to emphasise this more traditional interpretation which tells us that God asks us to sacrifice that which is dearest to us. My reason for playing it down is simply because the way in which it is frequently understood can be quite damaging. It plays into and supports a spirituality where God makes arbitrary demands – calling on us to perform actions which are not only irrational but even, perhaps, immoral. For instance, it made me sad to hear that Gerard Manley Hopkins burned much of his poetry because he felt he should sacrifice what was dearest to him. So, for me, it seems wiser not to stress this 'ultimate sacrifice' notion. Perhaps it is better to leave it to the Spirit of God to teach deeply spiritual people to discover where and when God is calling them to willingly let go of some person or project to which they have become unduly attached.

I find it better, for the most part, to suggest the following rather different interpretation of the story. We start by noting that in both the biblical and the Qur'anic accounts what we find are two messages from God. The first is the message to kill his son and the second is a message not to engage in such a human sacrifice. For me, the best way to understand this is to see the first message as one which has come through the traditional belief of the people among whom Abraham was living. At that time there was a widespread belief (not only in the Middle East but also in Greece and elsewhere) that in extreme circumstances the most effective way to placate or manipulate God or the gods is by a human sacrifice of a much-loved child. In the Abraham story there comes a second message from God – a last-minute command to spare his child. This represents a breakthrough in the history of religion. It is a most striking example of what I am calling a 'revelatory moment'. The new revelation is that Abraham's God is not the kind of cruel and demanding God who needs to be placated by human sacrifice.

It may be asked whether the interpretation which I have just proposed is true to the historical reality. In other words, did the first of these two 'commands' of God really come from Abraham's culture rather than directly from God as is commonly

assumed? In reply, I can only say that the truth of the story of
Abraham is mythic rather than literal. In fact, as I pointed out
earlier, we cannot even be sure that the story of Abraham's sacrifice is literally, historically, true. What matters is its reality as a
key part of the founding myth of three great religions – Judaism,
Christianity and Islam.

It is characteristic of myth that it has several layers of meaning; and the meaning depends largely on the context. In a new
situation the myth can take on a new and richer meaning – one
that is relevant to the new context. I suggest that in the light of
our present Christian understanding of God we cannot really
believe that God would demand that Abraham sacrifice his son
– even by way of testing his faith. On the other hand, it may
make more sense to Christians of our time to see the real significance of the story not in the command to Abraham to kill his son
but, on the contrary, in the last-minute command *not* to kill the
child.

Many of us may have a moment of revelation rather similar
to that of Abraham – a moment when we felt liberated from
what we had come to see as a superstitious belief. We may have
previously imagined that we could make a bargain with God or
could guarantee that we would gain some benefit by going
through some ritual – for instance by reciting some prayer on
nine successive days. Then one day we came to realise that we
cannot force the hand of God and that God doesn't make that
kind of bargain. (Recall my account of the difference between a
bargain and God's covenant in Chapter 4 above.)

As a Christian community, too, we have experienced such
moments of revelation and transformation. One example of
such a breakthrough took place forty years ago. It was a radical
change in the attitude of western Christians towards the peoples
of the traditional cultures of Africa, Australia and elsewhere. For
Catholics it came with the Second Vatican Council. For
Protestants it arose as a result of a key meeting of the World
Council of Churches. Prior to that time we used such terms as
'pagans' or 'unbelievers'. Missionaries and local preachers de-
manded that converts reject their traditional religious symbols
and burn them publicly. Nowadays, we refer to their religion in
more respectful terms such as 'primal religion'. We look for

ways in which Christian belief can welcome and enrich all that is good in these traditional beliefs and symbols. Furthermore, we now believe that we can come to a richer understanding of our Christian faith by taking account of the traditional beliefs of these peoples.

Dare I suggest that we in the Catholic Church now need a further revelatory breakthrough? It is one which will enable us to correct some of the unduly exclusive demands which we have assumed that God is making of us in regard to sharing Eucharist with other Christians and joint worship with people of non-Christian religions.

Fundamentalism

A final point about the Abraham story concerns the fanatical fundamentalism which can be found in extreme groups in each of the three great Abrahamic faiths. The Islamic version of the story has been read by a small but significant number of Muslims in a way that provides them with a basis for an extreme religious fanaticism. The hero of the story as told in the Qur'an is Abraham's older son, Ishmael, who is seen as the father of the Arab people and the ancestor of Muhammad. The Qur'an says that Ishmael was a willing victim, since he was the one who insisted that his father kill him in obedience to God's command. This reading of the Islamic version of the Abraham story is used by some extremists as an ideological-theological basis for suicide bombers.

On the other hand, the biblical account of God giving 'The Promised Land' to Abraham and his descendents provides an ideological basis for the religious fundamentalism of a small minority of extreme Jewish sects. It is a fanaticism which drives them to go against all reason, seeking to expel whole populations from land surrounding present-day Israel, on the basis of what they see as an authorisation by God to possess the promised land of 'Greater Israel'.

Similarly, the biblical story of Abraham may be understood as providing support to an extreme form of Christian fanaticism, where God authorises the killing of innocent people. Those who hold such a fanatical view have made common cause with political neo-conservatives in being willing to slaughter thousands of

civilians, and to torture suspected terrorists, in the fight against
the so-called 'axis of evil'.

Reconciliation
There is a biblical basis for an alternative to these kinds of fundamentalism – one which emphasises reconciliation rather than
fanatical opposition to the enemy. The Book of Genesis tells us
that when Abraham died he was buried by his two sons, Isaac
and Ishmael (Gen 25:9). So at this sad moment there was a coming together of these two sons of Abraham who had been so
cruelly separated as children and had become the ancestors of
the Jews and the Arabs. In recent years thousands of Jews and
Arabs have died in the on-going struggle between them. Should
we not see the story of the burial of Abraham as an invitation to
all believers in the God of Abraham to work together for a just
reconciliation where ancient quarrels are buried along with
those who have died in these tragic struggles? Should not such a
reconciliation be part of our deepest heart's desire?

CHAPTER EIGHT

The Calls of Moses, Esther and Judith

Though it is helpful to explore the call of Abraham, the focus in that story is so much on going forward in trust into the unknown that it leaves us with a lot of vagueness about what we might call 'the content' of the call – that is, what kind of commitments it involved. A study of the call of Moses, by contrast, gives a very specific insight into what it meant in practice for him to answer God's call. Consequently, it can throw light on what it means for each of us to respond to our own personal call.

When we look at the call of Moses we see that, like that of Abraham, it began with a vivid experience of God. And, for Moses as for Abraham, there was a background which prepared him for this experience. So we can begin by looking closely at this background.

Moses was a Jewish child who was adopted and reared as an Egyptian. He grew up situated between two cultures, half-way between the Egyptians and his own people. As a young adult he killed an Egyptian who was beating a Jew. This caused him to be rejected both by his own people and by the Egyptians (Ex 2:11-15). So he had to let go of home, of his possessions, and of his status as he fled into exile. He settled down as a refugee and foreigner in the land of Midian and married a local woman.

An Experience of God
As I have said, his call and his mission began with a theophany, a vivid experience of God. God declared: 'I am the God of your ancestors, the God of Abraham, the God of Isaac, and the God of Jacob' (Ex 3:6) – so there is continuity with the past: this is the ancestral God of Moses' own people. But something very interesting happens when Moses asks for the name of this God. God's response is 'I am' ('*eheyeh*') which is linked to the name 'Yahweh'. According to some recent scholarship this name

'Yahweh' appears to be the name used for God at that time by the local people (the Midianites). Using this local name 'Yahweh', God immediately identifies it with the God of the Jewish ancestors, Abraham, Isaac and Jacob (Ex 3:15).

For us Christians today, living as we do in an intercultural world, this has important implications. It suggests that we are called to learn more about the various Hindu deities as well as the local deities of the peoples who live in traditional primal cultures. Perhaps we should see it as an invitation for us to explore whether these deities can be understood as expressing some aspects or features of the God of the bible, the God revealed by Jesus Christ.

It is also significant that when Moses asks for the name of God, the name he is given is 'Yahweh' rather than the word 'Elohim', which had been used earlier (e.g. Ex 3:4). The name 'Yahweh' seems to have a more personal character than 'Elohim', which appears to be a more generic name for divinity. This suggests that Moses had a more personal relationship with God than those who went before him. In fact Moses seems to be the only one in the whole Old Testament who had such intimate contact with God. The biblical texts communicate very powerfully the power and the awe of that experience. The very ground around the burning bush is holy; and later on when Moses speaks with God his face becomes so radiant that he has to put a veil on it when speaking with mere humans (Ex 34:35).

I venture to quote some lines from the linked poems 'Burning Bush' and 'Mirror of Light' by Michael McCarthy – lines which convey something of this experience of being in the presence of God:

'…"Moses, Moses, Moses." It came like a mantra from the bush
As if someone were making music, borrowing my name.
"I'm here," I said, "I'm here." I didn't know what else to say.
It was then I took off my shoes,
to hear what the ground was saying.
My feet naked on the earth felt the calligraphy of grass …
I became bewildered then. "I am, I am."
That's all I can remember. "I'm here," I said.'
'… I said nothing then, there was no need for speech.

God's eyes, my eyes, within each other, seeing with one
    vision.
Together in our veins, in our measure of the mountain.
Moment by moment, we knew everything. ...
God breathing, into me, out of me, all in one river.
For three days a mirror of light.
"God", one word only. A whisper: "Moses".[1]

A Call to Liberation

Just as Abraham's call by God involves a mission, so too with
Moses. And as always, the authenticity and extent of his mission
is directly proportional to the depth of his experience of God.
Moses had such a vivid experience of God that it is no wonder
that his mission was equally dramatic and fundamental: 'I have
seen the misery of my people in Egypt. I have heard their cry ...
Go to Pharaoh ... and say: "Let my people go".' (Ex 3:7; 7:15-6)

Here in the encounter of Moses with God we have the basis
for a call to work for human liberation, which involves making
an option for the oppressed and the poor. Let me give a very
brief outline of what this involves. The first point to note is that a
prior condition for genuine liberation and option for the poor is
an experience of solidarity with those who are on the margins of
society.

Moses learned the painful lesson that it is not enough to be
looking down from above and trying to help oppressed people
without sharing their experience. While still in a privileged position he tried to take the side of the oppressed Jews. The result
was that he was no longer in favour with either the Egyptians or
the Jews, and he had to go into exile. It was only when he himself had lived as a refugee that he was able to come back as an
instrument of God to bring liberation to his people. If we as
Christians want to bring liberation to people, we too must share
in some degree the experience of those who are poor or disadvantaged or oppressed. A test of this is whether we make friends
with those on the margins of society – and to what extent we live
close to them geographically or at least psychologically, and
have an open house for them.

Moving on from solidarity with the poor and oppressed to

1. CD: "Birds' Nests and Other Poems", 1999.

making an option for them involves first of all ensuring that we are not colluding or acquiescing in patriarchy, sexism, racism, or the unjust political-economic system which creates such a gap between the rich and the poor. Next, we must seek to understand the basic causes of the oppression. Then, like Moses, we must look for effective ways of challenging the oppressive powers. And, again like Moses, we must make sure that we can offer people a realistic alternative to the situation of oppression.

Leadership
This mention of an alternative reminds us that the task given by God to Moses did not consist solely in getting his people out from under the domination of Egypt; he then had to lead them though the wilderness for many years and bring them within sight of the Promised Land. It is the same for people today who commit themselves to the task of liberation. Following on from that initial commitment is one where the task is one of accompanying people – perhaps in a leadership role – through years of wilderness and doubt, up to a point where they can get a glimpse of the new Land which God has promised.

They, like Moses, may often find it burdensome to carry through with these roles of accompaniment and, more particularly, of leadership. Moses found the task of leadership so demanding that eventually he had to take the advice of Jethro, his father-in-law, and get others to share the task (Ex 18:17-24). Those who, like him, find themselves in a leadership role must develop ways of sharing that leadership with others. Then they will face the excitement and challenge of exercising team leadership. At times they will be exasperated with the people around them, as Moses was when the Jews seemed to be abandoning their God to follow idols. And there will be times, too, when the people are exasperated with their leaders. In some situations of great doubt or crisis, would-be leaders may find that, like Moses, there is nothing else they can do except pray desperately to God on behalf of the people with whom they have chosen to be in solidarity (Ex 17:9-12).

Like Moses, these would-be leaders probably don't – and won't – often have the joy and excitement of actually leading their people into the new world that has been promised. They generally have to settle for leading people to the point where that new world is still over the horizon and can only be glimpsed in privileged moments. But there is consolation in that too. It scales down the expectations of those who have taken on a leadership role. They don't have to think that they have failed in answering to God's call if the people they work with have not yet fully entered into the land of promise, and have not yet fully experienced all that God has in store for them.

Esther

One of the key points in the story of Moses is that, in his call, the vertical and the horizontal aspects of spirituality come together. The vertical aspect is Moses' intimate relationship with God; the horizontal aspect is his call to lead his people out of slavery into their own land. This conjunction of the two dimensions lies at the heart of any genuine spirituality. Down through history many people have made the mistake of focusing solely or primarily on the vertical dimension. Time after time in the bible the prophets warn their people that what pleases God is not ritual sacrifices but concern for justice and mercy (e.g. Is 6:6).

Many centuries after the time of Moses two interesting stories were added to the biblical literature. Each of them centres on the exploits of a brave woman. In the stories of Esther and of Judith we find once again an inextricable link between their relationship with God and their concern to rescue their people. And this link is very evident in the prayer which each of them makes before setting out to face the enemy. Furthermore, the stories bring out clearly that these two women believe that in taking on the task of rescuing their people they must depend utterly on God. Of course they have to steel themselves to do their part, risking their lives. But all the time they see themselves simply as pliant instruments in the hand of God.

Esther is a Jewish woman who, during the time of the Babylonian captivity, has been taken into the harem of King Ahasuerus and made his queen. The story tells us that at this time all the Jewish people are to be destroyed. Esther's cousin, Mordecai, who had reared her, challenges her to plead with the king on behalf of her people. 'Who knows', says Mordecai, 'perhaps you have come to the throne for just such a time as this.'

(Esther 4:16). To come before the king means taking her life in her hands, since death is the penalty for anybody who approaches him without being called by the king himself.

Esther turns to God in earnest prayer. Then, fortified by this prayer, she works out her strategy. There are two stages in it. In the first step she ventures into the king's presence and invites him to a meal. In the second stage she uses all her feminine charms on him before begging him to spare her life and that of her people. All turns out well. In fact Haman, the chief enemy of her people, is hanged on the scaffold which he had built for the execution of Mordecai (Esther 7:10).

Judith

In the story of Judith it is once again a brave woman who single-handedly rescues her people from destruction. Her town of Bethulia has been besieged by the army of the Assyrian general Holofernes and its water supply has been cut off. The elders of the town decide that they will, so to speak, give God one more chance to save them. So they set a time-limit: if help does not come within the next five days, they will surrender to their enemies (Judith 7:31-2).

Judith openly challenges this decision. In a stirring speech (Judith 8:11-27) she takes on these male leaders and becomes their teacher in relation to the true relationship between God and humanity. The kernel of her argument is that we must put no limits to our trust in God: 'Who are you to put God to the test?' She shows remarkable spiritual insight when she says that we dare not imagine that we can know the purposes of God. 'If we cannot even know the human mind how can we imagine that we know the mind of God? ... Our place is not to put God to the test by setting a time-limit for an intervention by God ... God is not to be threatened as a human being, nor is God to be cajoled, like a mere human. Rather we must simply await God's good pleasure, entrusting ourselves into the caring hands of God.'

Judith then backs up her words by her actions. She proves her total trust in God by undertaking to overcome the enemy general. Before she ventures out to do so she, like Esther, turns to God in earnest prayer, recalling that Yahweh is the God of the weak, the poor, and the humble (Judith 9:1-14). Fortified by this prayer she goes out with only her maid – and eventually she succeeds in killing the enemy general Holofernes with his own sword.

It is quite likely that in the patriarchal context of biblical times the point of the stories of Esther and Judith was thought to be that even women could be instruments of God, since what matters is not human strength but God's action. In our time, however, we can read a stronger meaning into these stories. We can see both stories as reminders to us that, even when men fail in their God-given tasks, women can hold on, can challenge the men, and can prove their case by being effective instruments of salvation for their people.

From the point of view of our own spirituality, it is important to note that the personal call of Esther did not come directly from God as did that of Moses. Rather God's call was mediated through a strong plea and call from Mordecai, her cousin and the leader of her people.

Even more interesting is the call of Judith to risk her reputation by challenging the male leaders, and to risk her life by going out alone against the foreign general. In her case the call was sparked off by the failure of the leaders to put their total trust in God. This called forth the faith and trust of her own heart, a trust that was clearly the central reality in her life. The ways in which God called these two women find echoes in our own lives. We do not have wait to see a burning bush; the Spirit is already calling us through the needs, the pleas, and the weaknesses of those around us – and in the wider world.

CHAPTER NINE

The Call of Jesus

We come now to the call of our fifth biblical figure, and this time it is Jesus. The gospels suggest that the public mission of Jesus, like the mission of Abraham and Moses, began with a theophany – a vivid experience of God. In his case this was his baptism, where he experienced himself as 'The Beloved of God' and as filled and empowered and led by God's Spirit (Mt 3:16-7). Implicit in this experience was his call and his mission, which was to share with everybody else a similar sense and conviction of being the beloved of God. Above all he felt called to share this experience with those on the margins of society – the poor, the sick, the rejected ones and those who were seen as public sinners.

The mission of Jesus was in direct continuity with the liberating mission of Moses. However, the call and the mission of Jesus went deeper. Going beyond a concern for political oppression and economic impoverishment, Jesus challenged the internalised oppression which causes people to believe that they are not loved by God and are of no value. For instance, he showed special concern for the lepers who were generally assumed to be cursed or punished by God, and who would themselves have come to accept that view of their illness.

From the moment of his baptism up to the end of his life Jesus was constantly led by the Spirit. The first place where the Spirit led him was into the wilderness. The gospels describe how he was tempted there by the devil (Mt 4:1-10; Lk 4:1-13). These temptations can be understood as a time which Jesus devoted to discerning how best to carry out his mission. The kernel of his discernment was concerned with the way he should use his power. Tempted to impress people by ostentatious miracles or to overwhelm them through power, he opted instead to relinquish that kind of oppressive power. Instead he chose to spread his good news by taking the side of those who were poor and despised and by living in solidarity with them. He decided that this was the most appropriate and effective way to convince them that each of them is the beloved of God.

The Title he gave himself

Perhaps the most striking indication of how he saw his mission was the title he chose to use for himself. More than seventy times in the New Testament Jesus called himself, or is described as, 'The Human One' – that is a more accurate translation of the phrase usually translated as 'The Son of Man'.

By choosing this title rather than a title like 'The Messiah', Jesus was, first of all, emphasising his humanity, saying that he is one of us, in solidarity with all other humans in the world. Secondly, in the light of the way this phrase is used in the Book of Daniel (7:13-4), the title implied that Jesus is in some way a mysteriously special kind of person. He can perhaps be seen as a model for what it means to be human – even as a representative of all humanity and the fulfilment of humanity's highest purposes. Thirdly, the fact that Jesus called himself 'the Human One' tells us that the way to come close to God is not to try to escape from this world or to run away from everyday human issues and problems but rather to live fully authentic human lives. Anybody who wants to live a truly human life is committed to resisting everything that dehumanises people anywhere, because Jesus shows that the way to God is through being fully human.

All this gives a clear mandate to us who see ourselves as called to share the good news of Jesus. Jesus, the Human One, invites us to live an authentically human life as he did – and to empower others to do the same. This means living by the values of justice, compassion, ecological sensitivity, and all the other ethical values; and of course it also means living contemplatively in the presence of God. For Jesus, and his followers, the vertical and the horizontal dimensions of spirituality meet and overlap. So, a crucial aspect of our call is to help people accept that to have an authentic relationship with God and Jesus they must devote themselves to both of these aspects. They must not understand spirituality solely in terms of their relationship with God or their personal experience of the transcendent, but must be fully committed to respecting all fellow-humans and caring for the earth.

I have written elsewhere[1] about how Jesus lived his life: his warm human friendships and his care for the outcasts, as well as his challenge to the rich and powerful, to religious oppression and authoritarianism, to legalism, and to patriarchy. So here I move straight on to some of what we can learn from the way Jesus faced the darkness at the end of his life.

Dismayed and crushed by rejection and betrayal, he gathered his friends around him first at a ritual meal and then as he prayed in the garden. He showed his weakness and vulnerability and begged his closest friends to support and watch with him. This suggests that we, his followers, should be in touch with our own vulnerability and not be reluctant to show that vulnerability to others.

Four Different Viewpoints

The four gospels give us four rather different accounts of the passion and death of Jesus. In the early church there were some attempts to turn them into one fully coherent narrative. But Christians came to realise that this attempt at harmonisation was a mistake, since the differences are quite significant. It may be helpful for us to explore the differences.[2]

In Mark's gospel (Mk 14:32-15:39) Jesus comes across as a broken man. He falls flat on his face in the garden and prays in vain to be spared from the great ordeal that is before him. Each time he comes to look for support from his friends he finds they have let him down by falling asleep. Dying on the cross, he experiences himself as let down and abandoned not merely by his friends by also by God. In this gospel, it is only after his death that Jesus is vindicated by God – as is shown by the tearing of the curtain of the Temple and the recognition by the Roman soldier that this was 'a son of God'.

According to Mark's gospel (Mk 15:34), Jesus on the cross

1. *Divine Energy*, Dublin: Gill and Macmillan, 1996, and Liguori, Missouri: Triumph, 1996, pp 58-85.
2. I rely here on Raymond Brown's masterful treatment of this topic in *The Death of the Messiah*, New York and London: Doubleday, 1994, especially Vol I, 26-35; Vol II, 1018, 1049, 1066-78.

cried out in anguish to God, 'Why have you abandoned me?' (In fact, the text, translated literally, says that he 'screamed' those words.) Down through the ages and right up to the present day many scholars have played down or re-interpreted the text, arguing that God could not have abandoned Jesus. It would seem that they have failed to take sufficient account of the huge difference between *feeling* abandoned by God and *being* abandoned.

Matthew's description of the passion (Mt 26:36-27:56) is quite similar to that of Mark, though just a little softer. His account also stresses the fact that, while his own people rejected him, outsiders such as Pilate's wife could recognise that Jesus was an innocent man.

There is quite a different tone to the account of Jesus' passion in Luke's gospel (Lk 22:39-33:48). Here Jesus remains in control throughout his passion. In the garden, he does not fall on his face but kneels upright as he prays. God answers his prayer by sending an angel to comfort him. When he finds his friends sleeping, he does not seem to experience this as an abandonment by them but sees them as worn out by grief. He heals the man whose ear had been cut off. He tells the women of Jerusalem to weep not for him but for themselves and their children. He prays for forgiveness for those who crucified him. He promises paradise to 'the good thief'. And his final words are: 'Into your hands I commit my spirit.'

John's account (Jn 18:1-19:37) contrasts quite sharply with the story as told by Mark and Matthew; and John goes much further than Luke in emphasising the extent to which Jesus remained fully in control. Here we find a Jesus who never falters in doing his Father's will. He looks forward eagerly to his ultimate confrontation with evil. As he had said earlier:

> I lay down my life in order to take it up again. No one takes it from me; I lay it down of my own free will. I have authority to lay it down, and I have authority to take it up again.
> (Jn 10:17-18)

He steps forward confidently to meet those who come to arrest him – and they fall to the ground when he confronts them. Telling Peter to put up his sword, he assures him that he is perfectly willing to drink the cup of suffering prepared for him. He does not hesitate to challenge his captors when he is accused of being disrespectful to the high priest. In his dialogue with Pilate it appears that it is not Jesus but Pilate who is on trial. And as he dies on the cross he can proclaim that his task has been accomplished. All through, his death is seen as his triumph.

Implications for Spirituality
We may feel inclined to ask which of these accounts is the most accurate, the nearest to what actually happened. But this is not a helpful question. It is better to recognise that each of the four evangelists has his own distinctive theology. None of them is offering a baldly factual account of the details of the suffering and death of Jesus. Instead, each of them is giving an account in which the historical details are adapted to meet a particular interpretation of the story. These different interpretations depend to a considerable extent on the particular time-period when each gospel was composed, and on the situation of the young Christian communities where the gospels were written. The result is that what the gospels give us is four different perspectives on a truth that is larger than any one of them.

From the point of view of our spirituality, the question 'Why have you abandoned me?' in the gospels of Mark and Matthew, is quite important. So too is the distinction between *feeling* abandoned by God and *being* abandoned. Many deeply committed people go through a 'dark night' experience or find themselves at times in such deep depression that they may *feel* quite abandoned even by God. For them to know that Jesus had a similar experience may give them encouragement to 'hang on' in the hope that their mood will lighten and they will once again feel that God cares for them. As Gerard Manley Hopkins says in one of his poems:

> Not, I'll not, carrion comfort, Despair, not feast on thee;
> Not untwist – slack they may be – these last strands of man
> In me or, most weary, cry I can no more. I can;
> Can something, hope, wish day come, not choose not to be.

When we are facing a difficult situation or some ultimate test, we are likely to find that at different moments one or other of the four gospel accounts of Jesus' passion may find an echo in our own experience. At one moment we may feel broken and abandoned, as Jesus did in the accounts of Mark and Matthew. But then we may find that even in that brokenness we still have some degree of freedom. We can move beyond our sense of abandonment and reach out in concern to others, as Jesus did according to Luke's account.

There may even come a time when we discover deep within us something of that high degree of inner freedom which Jesus shows in John's gospel. In that frame of mind we remain, despite the external restrictions, in full command, under God, of our destiny.

All of these experiences and perspectives are aspects of the truth. For much of the time we may find within us a mixture of all of them. It is very reassuring for us to know that in any or all of them we can be following Jesus, who was fully human like ourselves. He shared our human life-experience to the full, including our brokenness and sense of abandonment.

There are other things, too, that we can learn from the accounts of his passion. When his disciples let Jesus down, he then went on alone to face the powers of evil. Realising that he was being scapegoated in the trials before the Sanhedrin and Pilate, he unmasked by his judicious use of words and of silence the self-deception that is the core of the scapegoating process.

There is much to be said for the view that Jesus consciously took on the role of the Suffering Servant who bears our suffering and whose wounds bring us healing (Is 53:1-12). He did this by allowing the evil of hatred and rejection to have its way with him. Then, through the power of his forgiveness and love, he transformed that evil energy into a powerful healing and redeeming energy which radiates out from him through space and time.

The resurrection of Jesus is the vindication by God of the redemptive work of Jesus. The experience of the disciples on the road to Emmaus is particularly revealing (Lk 24:13-35). It shows us that, for those who have received the gift of faith, the resurrection of Jesus completes the pattern of redemption, making sense of all that has gone before.

Our Share in his Work

Jesus enables us to share in his redemptive work not just by modelling how we are to act but by allowing us 'to fill up what is lacking in his sufferings' (Col 1:24). From Jesus we learn how to unmask the scapegoating engaged in by ourselves or others. Then we go on to share with Jesus the healing and redemptive role of Suffering Servant. As Christians we are privileged to play a key role in radiating outwards the healing and redemptive power of Jesus' love. With utmost respect we can invite others to respond to the promptings of the Spirit of Jesus and to take on that role of transforming hatred into healing and redeeming energy.

In difficult times we may be tempted to doubt the reality and efficacy of our human role in spreading, and adding to, the redemptive love of Jesus. How then can we nourish and renew our faith in that power? One way of doing so is by reflecting prayerfully on the lives of those who have gone before us – saints whose loving influence on others can scarcely be doubted. We can also learn from the spiritual practices of other religions. For instance, we can borrow from the Buddhist tradition the 'Loving Kindness Meditation' which is a very effective way of cultivating a personal sense of the healing and redemptive power of love in our lives.

Faith in Jesus

At the end of Chapter 5 above I suggested that our part in having faith in God means, in practice, making a leap of hope – acting as if God is benevolent and provident. But what does it mean to have faith in Jesus? How is it different from having faith in, say, a good doctor or a reliable friend? For me, the answer is that it may sometimes happen that even an excellent doctor makes a mistake and even the most reliable friend may occasionally let me down. This means that my faith in the doctor or the friend cannot be utterly unconditional.

In contrast to this, there are no conditions or reservations in regard to my faith in Jesus. I never find myself asking: 'Could Jesus have been wrong in the way he handled some situation recounted in the gospel?' Furthermore, if I conclude that Jesus is calling me to act in a particular way, my subsequent doubts or hesitations are not about whether that course of action might be wrong, but only about my own judgement or about my ability to follow the call.

However, faith in Jesus only makes sense when it is suffused with love. Central to that faith is an acceptance that love is the ultimate power in our lives and in the world; and that, by God's grace, love can transform even the suffering caused by evil, giving it a redemptive quality. This means that we are called to have, at the heart of our Christian spirituality, a commitment to believe in, to trust, and to nourish this kind of redemptive love. Consequently, one element in our deepest heart's desire should be a longing for what might be called a personal 'Emmaus experience'. By this I mean the kind of enlightenment which enables us to say: 'Was it not necessary that he [and we] suffer these things and so enter into glory?' (Lk 24:26).

CHAPTER TEN

The Call of Mary

In this chapter I want to look at Mary – or more specifically at the Magnificat, the prayer which St Luke in his gospel puts in the mouth of Mary (Lk 1:46-55). The first thing to note is that this beautiful prayer extends over a period of sixty or seventy years. Its location in the gospel is when Mary visits her cousin Elizabeth some months prior to the birth of Jesus. But the words of the prayer were actually written down by the evangelist per- haps thirty or forty years after the death of Jesus. How can we hold this together? I suggest that we see the present text of the Magnificat as an unfolding and spelling out by Luke of senti- ments that were present in germ in an unarticulated way many years previously in the heart and mind of Mary.

By the time Luke wrote down this prayer there had been at least sixty years during which both Mary and Luke had ample time to have had the kind of 'Emmaus experience' which I re- ferred to at the end of the previous chapter. Such an experience is a kind of personal revelation, bringing a rich new insight into how the whole story of our salvation hangs together.

In fact we can take it that Mary's prayer during her later life was underpinned by such an experience. But for her it would not have been just a once-off event but rather an on-going and ever deepening vision of how God's plan had worked out in the life and death and resurrection of Jesus – and of her own role in that plan. Furthermore, this retrospective understanding of hers would embrace all that had led up to the mission of Jesus, going right back to the creation of the world and including the promise made to Abraham and the role of Moses in the liberation of God's people.

Her Proclamation – and Ours
So, let us now picture Mary in her old age looking back with

new insight, with enriched understanding, with boundless gratitude, and in a spirit of joyful celebration, on how that history had unfolded according to the plan of God. Her first instinct is to cry out in praise of God:

My whole being proclaims the greatness of the Almighty
and my spirit rejoices in God my Saviour,
who has remembered me, a lowly servant of God.

This is followed at once by her recognition of the amazing gifts which God has given her and a clear-sighted acknowledgement that future generations will recognise and declare that she has been blessed by God:

From this time onward people of all ages will call me blessed
because of the marvels done for me
by God whose name is holy.

We who read and pray these words are invited by them to do what Mary did – to look back on our own lives and beyond, to see how the plan of God has been fulfilled in what we have done and in what has happened to us. If we do it with faith we should find ourselves marvelling like Mary at the wonders God has done for us.

This invitation extends to all of us, but it may perhaps be particularly relevant to older people. Some of the readers of this book, or their friends, are probably now retired or semi-retired from fulltime work. To retire from a job or from fulltime active ministry does not mean that one has ceased to be spiritually engaged and active. We remain fulltime Christians for all of our lives.

My hope is that all of us – and especially those who are no longer on full-time active service – will, like Mary, have what may be called 'a Magnificat experience'. That would mean rejoicing in God as we look back with utter gratitude on the gifts we have received all during our lives. It would involve recognising how blessed we have been in so many different ways. Hopefully, it would even lead us to a rather diffident acknowledgement and rejoicing that at least some of the people who have worked with us or known us will remember us as privileged instruments of God.

The Theme of Liberation

As Mary looks back to the time of Moses and the prophets who came after him, she gets a new appreciation for the whole theme of liberation of the poor and the oppressed. She says:

> The All-powerful One has stretched out a mighty arm,
> to foil the plans of the arrogant,
> to pull down mighty rulers from their seats of power,
> and lift up the little people.
> God has filled the hungry with the best of food
> while the rich are sent away empty.

In this passage – and indeed in much of the rest of the Magnificat – there seems to be a quite deliberate borrowing of the words put in the mouth of Hannah, mother of the last of the judges who ruled in Israel before the kingship was established (1 Sam 2:1-10). This signals the place of Mary's prayer as a bridge between the Old Testament and the new era ushered in by Jesus. It reminds us particularly of how the theme of liberation, which runs right through the earlier history of the Jewish people, has come to full fruition with the coming of Mary's child, Jesus. Reflecting on that history, both at the actual time of her pregnancy and many years later, Mary is proclaiming her faith that God will continue to be on the side of the poor and those who have little or no earthly power. And her faith is strengthened as she recalls instances of God's power, shining through human weakness, in the history of her people and in her own life.

We, who see in Mary a model of authentic spirituality, are invited to look back on our lives and find there the same pattern of liberation as Mary outlines in this prayer. As we recall how our lives have unfolded, we have the opportunity to savour noteworthy occasions when we became aware of God's power. We may remember times when the arrogant and the mighty were discomforted and when those on the margins of society came to play a pivotal role or were given a privileged place. Perhaps, too, we may look back at times when we ourselves were able to co-operate with God in giving priority to people who were poor or despised, rather than kowtowing to the wealthy and the powerful.

Our spirituality is nourished by this kind of prayerful reflection on human history in general, on the history of the country or region where we have lived, and perhaps especially on our own personal history. It gives us the opportunity to reaffirm and strengthen our deepest heart's desire – to ensure that what we find most meaningful and reassuring in life is an awareness of how God has blessed us, rather than putting our meaning and hope in our own achievements. Those who are no longer in full-time active work may find it particularly helpful. For them it can be an effective way of countering the regrets about the past and the sense of having failed or being useless which sometimes trouble older people.

Fulfilment of the Promise

The final stanza of Mary's Magnificat is one in which she looks back even beyond the time of Moses – back to the promise made to Abraham. She sees, and rejoices in, the fulfilment of that promise down through the ages:

> God is the One who in the past
> came to the help of the people of Israel, God's people,
> fulfilling the promise made to those who went before us,
> a promise of mercy made by God to Abraham (and Sarah)
> and their children's children down through the ages.

These words of Mary's prayer in the gospel are an invitation to all of us to pray for, to expect, and to actively look for a similar experience of the fulfilment of God's promise in our own lives. This invitation may be especially relevant for older people and for anybody who has retired from fulltime active work. God's promise of personal fulfilment and of spiritual fruitfulness was implicit in the very first inklings they had that God was inviting them to live lives of active Christian service in the secular world, or in a religious community, or in some church ministry. It was made explicit whenever they said the beautiful prayer based on lines from Psalm 16: 'You, God, are my portion and my cup; it is you who will restore my heritage to me.' Now is a time when they can look back with gratitude as they experience the fulfil-ment of the promise.

Sharing Spiritual Experiences

The gospel account of the meeting between Mary and Elizabeth is very touching. Here we see two women, each of whom has had a profound spiritual experience. Coming together, they share with each other the encounter each of them has had with God. Their meeting and dialogue enriches both of them and deepens their response to the marvellous events that have changed their lives. So their sharing has become a further deep spiritual experience for each of them – this time one that is shared.

The lesson for us is obvious. Of course it is important that each of us has a deeply personal encounter with God, as the mystery that envelops our lives; and it is important that we reflect quietly on such experiences to ensure that we draw out their full significance. But this enrichment can be brought to an entirely new level if we have the privilege of encountering somebody who has had a similar or analogous experience. What emerges is not just new light on our own experience and an insight into the spirit-life of the other. The sharing is itself a new and exceptionally powerful spiritual experience, one which touches deep parts of the soul.

This kind of spiritual sharing is a very important element in living out our spirituality. So much so that the desire for a soul-friend (*anam-chara* in the Irish language) should be part of our deepest soul's desire. This is a point to which I shall return in the next chapter. Meanwhile, I just note that the mutuality of sharing with a soul-friend can give us a sense of what human community is intended by God to be. Through it we can get an inkling and a foretaste of 'what eye has not seen, and ear has not heard, what has not entered the human heart, what has been prepared for those who love God.' (1 Cor 2:9)

But is the Story True?

It is widely recognised that the early chapters of Luke's gospel are written in a literary form or mode which is radically different from the modern understanding of history. So the question arises whether the account of the meeting between Mary and Elizabeth is a true story. The answer depends on how we define the word 'true'. Biblical scholarship suggests that it is quite unlikely that Luke's account is a factually accurate record of a particular historical event. But that does not prevent it being true in a different and deeper sense.

Nobody imagines that the stories told by Jesus of 'The Prodigal Son' or 'The Good Samaritan' are true in a literal or factual sense. But they express profound spiritual realities which ring true in our own experience. Taking this a bit further, we can now accept that the Old Testament stories of Esther, Judith, Jonah and Tobias were never intended to be historically accurate accounts. Nevertheless, they were designed to lead us into important truths about God and ourselves. Much the same may be true of the stories told in the early chapters of Luke's gospel.

Written very many years after the event it is describing, the account of the meeting between Mary and Elizabeth gives us a deep insight into how the early Christians had come to understand God's plan of salvation. Hearing or reading this story, the Christians of that period would have been touched and moved, just as Mary and Elizabeth were in the story of their meeting. Relating the story to their own life experiences, these early Christians could echo the outpouring of wonder and gratitude expressed so eloquently by the two women in the story.

That story has been passed down to us through the centuries. It comes to us with the same freshness as when it was first written. It can put us in touch with a deep truth about what is really happening in the world, behind the appearances. It reveals to us how God is at work in our world and in each of us. In this sense, the account of the meeting of Mary and Elizabeth as told in Luke's gospel is a profoundly true story.

PART III

Spirituality and Morality

I don't want your sacrifices – I want your love;
I don't want your offerings – I want you to know me.
Isaiah 6:6

CHAPTER ELEVEN

A Spirituality of Intimacy

As humans we do not live in isolation. Most of our everyday life is lived through relationships with others, either in an interpersonal way with individuals or small groups, or in the more public sphere through our involvement in the life of our own nation and the wider world. It is obvious that our spirituality has an impact on all of these relationships – and that the relationships in turn affect how we live out our spirituality. In this third section of the book I shall look at a wide range of these relationships, covering topics where moral values and moral action are a crucial aspect of an authentic spirituality. I shall begin by looking at interpersonal relationships in the present chapter, leaving over to later chapters our involvement in public affairs.

My intention here is to focus, not on our more casual everyday interactions with others, but specifically on our relationships with those who are closest to us. That is why I decided to call the chapter 'A Spirituality of Intimacy'. In the first section of the chapter I shall look at the topic of deep friendship. Then I shall add something about the particular form of friendship which also involves a fully active sexual relationship between committed partners. Finally, I shall go on to the question of intimacy with God.

Soul-Friends

I am not aware that friendship is given a prominent place in most of the books and articles about spirituality. This is regrettable, because deep friendships can play such an important part in our spirituality. It is quite significant that two close friends, a man and a woman, stand as the founding figures of at least five of the great traditions of spirituality in the Catholic Church: Benedict and Scholastica; Francis of Assisi and Claire; Teresa of Avila and John of the Cross; Vincent de Paul and Louise de Marillac; Francis de Sales and Jane Frances de Chantal.

The most important thing I want to say about friendship is that at its deepest it goes beyond support and comradeship and camaraderie. It is about intimacy. It is a meeting of souls.

In the Irish Christian tradition the *anam-chara* (soul-friend) was an important figure. This was somebody with whom one could share one's very soul. There are two rather different categories of person with whom I can open up in this way, revealing what is most personal and intimate in my life.

The first of these is a spiritual director or guide, or a personal spiritual guru. My relationship with this guide is an unequal one. There is not, normally, a mutual or two-way sharing of deep secrets. The focus is very much on *my* spiritual journey. The guide or director is fully present to me, with the specific purpose of helping me to articulate what is happening in my life and to have a better sense of where God is leading me.

In this sense, the relationship is a professional one. I go to this director because I see him or her as in some sense a trained expert, a person who has learned how to do this difficult and challenging work. Down through the ages, the value of such a relationship has been recognised, not only within the Christian tradition but also in various other religions and spiritual traditions. Much has been written about it; and training programmes for spiritual directors have been devised and are widely available.

It is more interesting, in some ways, to look at the other kind of person with whom I can reveal my soul. This is a close personal friend. The relationship here is not a professional one – even if the friend happens to have been trained in spiritual direction. In this case there is an equality, a two-way opening up, where the friend reciprocates my sharing – either immediately or perhaps at some later time. The kind of self-revelation that is involved here goes far deeper than that which exists between work colleagues, team-mates, and what we might call 'social friends'. Quite frequently it is both more profound and different in tone from the sharing that occurs within families. In fact one may experience it as a particular gift from God if a member of one's own family becomes a soul-friend. Needless to say, there are various degrees of friendship – and even degrees of soul-friendship. I am focusing here on intense soul-friendships, because of the remarkable way in which they can deepen one's spirituality.

Timeless

One of the ways in which a meeting between soul-friends of this kind differs from a meeting with a spiritual director is that the clock seems to become irrelevant. These friends are likely to be oblivious of the time. There always seems to be more to share, no matter how long the dialogue goes on. Furthermore, the communication often takes place in ways that go beyond words. As Kahlil Gibran says in *The Prophet*: 'Without words, in friendship, all thoughts, all desires, all expectations are born and shared ... for in the dew of little things the heart finds its morning and is refreshed.'

With a spiritual director one looks for clarity and some degree of guidance. But sharing with a friend has no other purpose than the joy of being heard, of hearing the other, and of the new creation that emerges in the sharing. We are rescued from the practical, almost utilitarian, thinking which is the basis for so much of our everyday interpersonal communication.

I recall here the sharing of Mary and Elizabeth which I described in the previous chapter. What happens when two such friends share deep spiritual experiences is more than just a deeper understanding by both of them of their own experiences, and new insight into the spirit-life of the friend. There is also the emergence of something new – a dismantling of barriers so that the two souls seem to have touched each other. On very special occasions it may go even further. Personal boundaries may seem to dissolve to a point where it seems there is almost a merging of souls. What happens could be compared in some respects to a mystical experience.

Trust and Acceptance

Soul-friends love each other. But perhaps what defines the relationship between them is not so much their love as their trust of each other. Each time they share deeply, that trust grows. This growth in trust deepens the connection with the other person and opens each of them up to give and receive nourishment for the soul. Furthermore, even apart from its value in this particular relationship, increased trust brings about a change in the way a person approaches other people and other situations. It makes this person more open and transparent.

Inevitably, this leaves the person rather more vulnerable. The one whose defences are down will sometimes be wounded by the insensitive words or behaviour of others. But this may be seen as a relatively small price to pay for not having to approach each new situation in an over-cautious and calculating manner. In any case, the high degree of inner freedom which comes from being open and trusting makes it easier for the person to cope with hurts inflicted by others.

We often hear the phrase 'love is blind'. This is not true in the case of the kind of friendship I am describing. Each of the friends is likely to be fully aware of the limitations and faults of the other. But, far from damaging the friendship, this may actually deepen it. For the inadequacies of the other are seen in a clear-eyed but non-judgemental way. It goes beyond mere tolerance to a loving acceptance, combined with a willingness to help the other in overcoming the fault – but only if the other wishes to do so.

This uncritical acceptance is perhaps the most remarkable and grace-filled aspect of such soul-friendship. It seems to come as pure gift, even to those who are quite critically-minded in other situations. It gives us an inkling of the total acceptance with which God loves each of us, exactly as we are.

It is no wonder, then, that Ben Sira (Sirach), the writer of the Book of Ecclesiasticus, says:

A loyal friend is a powerful defence:
whoever finds one has indeed found a treasure.
A loyal friend is something beyond price ...
A loyal friend is the elixir of life. *(Sir 6:14-16)*

Sexual Relationship

I move on now to consider the particular kind of soul-friendship in which the two friends are married or are living in a committed sexual partnership. The essential new element in this case is that the sexual element adds love with the body to friendship at the level of soul. This is no minor addition. For we are bodily creatures, so we are spontaneously inclined to express our love and trust through our bodies.

In our everyday interactions with people we have reservations regarding the extent to which we allow ourselves to be touched – and we even react when somebody comes into our 'air-space'. We have much stronger built-in inhibitions about being naked in the presence of others. Our sexuality provides us with inclinations which, in particular circumstances, counterbalance these reservations and inhibitions. It even gives us what we may call a 'built-in guide' on when and how to touch others and let ourselves be touched.

When two soul-friends are involved in an active sexual relationship with each other, each of them is willing to be naked before the other – a nakedness of the body which gives expression to a total openness of soul and spirit, a desire to be utterly transparent to the other. The touch of the other brings healing at a very deep level. And this, ideally, is a mutual experience, where the reciprocity leads both partners to ever greater degrees of trust, acceptance, and intimacy at every level.

Of course our sexuality can get distorted in various ways – mainly as a consequence of faulty up-bringing, or through lack of balance in the way we use it, and more particularly as a result of sexual abuse. I have written elsewhere about the damaging effects of shame and how it relates to sexual abuse.[1] So I shall confine myself here to looking at situations where one's sexuality has not become unduly distorted.

A soul-friendship which comes in the form of a full sexual relationship affects one's spirituality at a very deep level. It lifts one out of the preoccupation with self which is the normal state for many of us for much of the time – e.g. 'how am I feeling? do I like what is happening? what are others thinking of me?' For significant periods of time – sometimes for days on end – one is focused instead almost entirely on the other. One looks on the other with passion – not primarily a passion of wanting to possess the other but rather a passion of tenderness where one is entirely taken up with feeling for, and with, the other.

There may even be special moments when there seems to be a blurring of the distinction between oneself and the other. No wonder, then, that both the Old Testament and the New Testament speak of the two partners becoming 'one flesh' (Gen 2:24; Mt 19:5).

1. *Time for a Change*, Dublin: Columba Press, 2004, pp 99-117

In the early stages of having fallen in love, one's experience of everyday life is changed quite radically. One seems to be lifted out of the humdrum reality of normal living and to exist instead in a world that sparkles with energy and excitement. With the passing of time the excitement dims. But ideally that does not mean that one has returned to a dull and commonplace state of existence. Instead, the exhilaration of early love becomes transformed into a quiet abiding sense of gratitude for being loved and trusted unconditionally. One has the assurance of being 'held', in a manner where the holding of the body gives expression to a deep acceptance at every level.

I need hardly say that all this is a deeply spiritual experience – one that brings enormous enrichment to a person's spirituality. So much so that one would have to conclude that a full sexual relationship is part of the normal way in which a person's spirituality flourishes. To decide that one will deliberately live a celibate life requires a special call. And this call does not mean that one is renouncing the experience of intimacy – for there is still the need for deep spiritual friendship, perhaps a greater need than ever. Furthermore, Christians who take a vow of celibacy are also committing themselves to giving extra energy and more time and attention to developing their intimacy with God – though this gives no guarantee that they will become more holy than others.

Intimacy with God

One might have thought that our relationship with God is such an unequal one that it would be impossible to have an experience of real intimacy with the divine. Nevertheless, the mystics assure us that it is possible – and many of us who would make no claim to being mystics have occasional experiences which give us at least some inkling of what it is like to be intimate with God.

It is true, of course, that if our relationship with God is an authentic one, we become deeply aware of our finitude, our helplessness, our sinfulness *vis-à-vis* the infinite love and power of God. We may want to cry out as the prophet Isaiah did: 'Woe is me! I am lost, for I am a person of unclean lips and I live among a people of unclean lips' (Is 6:5). Nevertheless, we can experience such a high degree of unconditional acceptance and love from

God that the gap between creator and creature seems to be bridged. Like Isaiah we may experience ourselves being touched by a burning coal. In his case the fire touched his lips, but in our case, the fire of God's love touches our heart.

For the mystics the intimacy with God is very intense – so powerful and vivid that they describe it as a sense of being taken out of themselves and of being in some degree merged with the divine. That is an ideal to which all of us may aspire. But the reality is that this is a gift of grace which is not given to very many of us.

For the rest of us, intimacy with God is usually a far less intense experience. When writing in chapter 4 about being present to God, I said that we allow our awareness to extend outward into the mystery that surrounds us. I must now add that for much of the time we may not have any vivid awareness of even this rather attenuated contact with God. Indeed, there may be long periods during which we may hardly experience any contact with the divine. It is more a matter of hanging on in faith than of having a vivid experience of God. In this situation, our faith at best takes the form of deep desire for communion with God. The words of the psalmist express this longing:

> O God, you are my God,
> for you I long,
> For you my soul is thirsting
> My body pines for you,
> like a dry weary land without water. (Ps 63:1)

However, our relationship with God is not confined to longing. There are moments when we do actually experience God's presence. They often come unexpectedly, perhaps at times when we would least expect them. Many people find that these moments of being touched by God do not come during their time of formal prayer, or at a time when they are consciously longing for God.

This is a point where intimacy with God differs significantly from the intimacy of soul-friendship except, perhaps, in the case of those who have mystical experiences. We do undoubtedly have a two-way experiential relationship with God. But for most of us, and for most of the time, it lacks the simultaneity which is characteristic of inter-human intimacy. By this I mean that at one time we are longing for God, reaching out for an experience of intimacy; but that is very often the time when God leaves us waiting in dryness. Then, 'out of the blue' we may become vividly aware of God's presence. At times it may come in the form of a surge of gratitude to God for the way events have turned out for us. And sometimes this sense of God's love simply steals into our consciousness without any obvious connection to what has been going on.

Why should it be that in our relationship with God we are so often deprived of the particular sense of fulfilment which is present when two people have come into deep communion with each other *at the same time*? Could it be that God is stretching us, inviting us to deepen our sense of need for God? Perhaps our awareness of God's absence is an invitation to extend our longing so that it permeates more of our everyday life, rather than being confined to moments of prayer. The uncertainty and questioning implied in the word 'perhaps' is important here. Perhaps what God wants most of all from us is that we engage in dialogue with God, questioning and exploring as we draw ever closer to this mystery which surrounds us, awaits us, and – almost incredibly – seeks intimate union with us.

CHAPTER TWELVE

Ecological Spirituality: Contemplative Aspect

I turn now to the topic of ecological spirituality. It has two aspects: a contemplative and nourishing dimension and a dimension of active commitment. I shall look at each of these in turn. I begin in this chapter with the contemplative side; and in the next chapter I shall move on to the active and practical side of an ecological spirituality.

It is not easy to describe the nourishing or contemplative aspect in words since it is mainly something that is experienced. I can only hope that the account I give here will strike a chord in the experience of the reader, since otherwise it will remain just empty words.

Most of us occasionally have the experience of meeting somebody who seems 'ungrounded', not quite knowing where they are, where they are going, or what they are looking for. Some people seem to live in that 'lost' or 'floating up in the air' state for much of their lives. The result is that their words carry little weight. We find it hard to give much credence to what they tell us or to rely on them. Other people, by contrast, give the impression that it is only very rarely that they feel 'lost' in this way. They are solidly anchored and grounded. They are reliable. What they have to say carries a certain conviction. We know where we stand with them.

It is quite significant that we use the word 'grounded' to describe people of this latter type. It suggests that a key way to avoid feeling lost and 'up in the air' is to establish a close connection with the earth. There are various ways to do this. Some people devote time and energy to gardening or to carpentry. Others find it helpful to go hill-walking or to go for a long walk – preferably alone – in an area where they experience nature in its pristine state.

A Way of Being
These practices can help one to foster an ecological spirituality. But more fundamental than these various activities is a certain attitude to the world around us – and even a certain way of being. It is a matter of having an on-going awareness that we are part of the great web of life, of experiencing ourselves as linked to the animals and the plants. Furthermore, it is helpful to know, not just in our heads but in a bodily manner, that we are an integral part of the wider cosmos – the mountains, the rivers, the seas, and even the stars and the galaxies. In recent years the phrase 'star-stuff' is being used increasingly to bring home to people that we humans, together with the animals, the plants, the world, the planets and the stars are all elements of a single fabric composed of waves and atoms and sub-atomic particles – all parts of one cosmos.

The sense of being in touch with the natural world will generally happen more or less automatically for traditional farmers and crafts-people. The kind of life they are living is a constant reminder to them that they are immersed in the web of life. But those of us who live in a technologically developed world can easily get cut off from our links with nature.

In Chapter 2 above, I quoted from Patrick Kavanagh's poem 'Canal Bank Walk' where he speaks of how the waters of the canal 'feed the gaping need' of his senses. It is significant that Kavanagh, who grew up in rural Ireland, nevertheless, when he came to live in Dublin, found a way to nourish his soul by sitting beside the canal. If we live in an urban area in the midst of a technological society it is still possible to remain in touch with the wonder and mystery of the natural world. But in that situation it has to be a conscious and deliberate process – exploring the most effective ways of keeping ourselves rooted and grounded in nature. As I pointed out earlier, the experience of being closely in touch with nature nourishes in us the virtues of *tranquillity*, *serenity*, and *groundedness*.

Humility
Humility is an important aspect of a genuine spirituality. Unfortunately, the word 'humility' is often understood very poorly. We can begin to recover the full richness of its meaning

by noting that the root word is *humus*, which means the ground or the earth. So, central to the meaning of the word 'humility' is the idea that one is 'grounded'. People who are 'grounded' or 'rooted' in the earth are conscious that they do not live in isolated independence. They are aware that they are part of the cycle of nature, dependent on the animals, the plants, and on the earth itself for food, water, shelter, and the air that they breathe.

Furthermore, people discover that they are dependent on the web of life not merely for nourishment for the body but also for the soul. They come to realise that, without a life-giving contact with nature, life becomes drab and work degenerates into drudgery. All this evokes in them a certain modesty which is an essential element in a true spirituality.

Our Relationship with God

From a Christian point of view, the most valuable aspect of an ecological spirituality is that, at its best, it rescues us from a conception of God as only transcendent and beyond the world. It enables us to come in touch with God as also within the world around us.

The authors of the Old Testament put great emphasis on God as being different from the world. They were reacting against the view, common at that time, that the world is part of God or is itself divine. However, the advance of science over the past few hundred years, and the perceived opposition between science and religion, has brought about an opposite danger in much of the Western world. For many people, the world around us has become emptied of its sacred character and God has been removed to a remote realm. Some assume that God has little or no influence on the world and a lot more have no conscious experience of contact with God in their everyday lives. This secularisation of the world and of human experience has brought about a serious spiritual impoverishment.

Within the past generation a growing minority of people in the West have become aware of how dull and pointless life becomes when it is emptied of a sense of the sacred. This has led to an attempt to re-sacralise the world. Quite a lot of people today have taken to speaking of the earth as 'Gaia', which is the name of the ancient Greek goddess of the earth. For some, the point of

ECOLOGICAL SPIRITUALITY: CONTEMPLATIVE

this is simply to emphasise that planet earth is a single interlocking system so that interference with the patterns of nature in one area can have unexpected damaging effects elsewhere. But, for others, the use of the term 'Gaia' is a deliberate return to the ancient primal or pagan belief that the world itself is divine. The difficulty with this approach from a Christian point of view is that God is no longer thought of as fully personal. This means that there is little or no room for prayer as a truly interpersonal relationship with God.

An authentically Christian spirituality has to hold in balance the two dimensions of God. On the one hand, there is the transcendent dimension. This means that God is distinct from the world and cannot be reduced to being just the world as a whole or some aspect of it; rather God is the creator of our universe. On the other hand – and equally important – is the immanent dimension, which means that God is present in our world and in every aspect of our lives.

A practical and effective way of holding the two together is to re-connect with the spirituality which was fostered by St Patrick and his followers in the evangelisation of Ireland. Prior to the coming of Christianity the people there had a vivid experience of the spiritual dimension of the world around them and of every aspect of life. For instance, every locality had its own sacred well; and practically every significant hill-top was a place of worship.

In the Celtic spirituality which emerged during and after the time of Patrick we find a truly fruitful integration of the transcendent and immanent dimensions of God. These Christians combined a warm personal devotion to God and to Jesus with belief that the natural world has a sacred character and provides us with an opening into the spiritual world. We get a sense of this in the ancient hymn variously known as 'The Breastplate of St Patrick' or as 'The Deer's Cry':

I arise today
Through the strength of heaven
Light of sun
Radiance of moon
Splendour of fire

Speed of lightning
Swiftness of wind
Depth of the sea
Stability of earth
Firmness of rock.
I arise today
Through God's strength to pilot me
God's eye to look before me
God's wisdom to guide me
God's way to lie before me
God's shield to protect me ...
Christ with me, Christ before me,
Christ behind me, Christ in me,
Christ beneath me, Christ above me,
Christ on my right, Christ on my left,
Christ when I lie down, Christ when I sit down,
Christ when I arise, Christ to shield me.
Christ in the heart of everyone who thinks of me,
Christ in the mouth of everyone who speaks of me.
I arise today.
(Translation by Kuno Meyer)

'The New Story'

'Have dominion over ... every living thing that moveth upon the face of the earth' (Gen 1:28, King James Version). These words have been used in the past to provide a religious justification for human exploitation of the animals, the plants, and the earth itself. In reaction to this, thinkers like Teilhard de Chardin and Thomas Berry and their followers have developed what Berry calls 'the New Story' of creation. They hold that our understanding of evolution can nourish our sense of God rather than undermining it.

This way of thinking and of experiencing the world is fundamental to a truly ecological spirituality. It means that we see God as working through the process of evolution. We may even visualise the Spirit of God hovering over the primeval waters, shaping the whole process of evolution, according to the creative, loving plan of God. However, we must not think of the Spirit as an external agent pushing and pulling from outside, but rather as intrinsic to the whole process, respecting it, while providing its creative energy, drawing forth complexity from more simple forms, and giving the process a pattern that makes life possible.

In all of this, God is no longer seen as 'the God of the gaps', the God who in the past was used to explain unusual or inexplicable events in our world such as lightning strikes or freak accidents. According to 'the New Story', God is not to be seen as 'intervening' from outside in our world, but rather as the primary creative cause who lies behind the process of evolution as a whole.

A genuinely ecological spirituality enables us to have a sense of God's personal loving care for each us, precisely because we experience God's presence in the web of life as a whole and in the very fabric of the world. We do not limit God's presence to our inner spiritual life, since we have a sense that God is equally at work in the 'public' world. As the poet Gerard Manley Hopkins says: 'The world is charged with the grandeur of God'.

When we allow ourselves to be nourished and refreshed spiritually by our contact with nature, and by 'the New Story' of creation, this deepens our awareness of what it means to be a co-creator with God. For we humans do not just contemplate nature and the world around us; we are also agents of change. We cultivate the soil, sow and harvest crops, plant flowers and trees, and rear domestic animals and pets. We also cut down trees to make furniture, drill for oil to heat our homes and to provide fuel for our motor cars. Some of us burn down equatorial forests, while others seek to prevent this destruction. Where does this human activity fit into our spirituality? In the next chapter, I shall try to answer that question by moving on from the contemplative and nourishing aspect of an ecological spirituality to its more active dimension.

CHAPTER THIRTEEN

Ecological Spirituality: Active Aspect

The very first chapter of the bible speaks of the relationship between humans and the world of nature. In almost all of the different translations the key words are 'subdue the earth' and 'be masters of ... all the living creatures' (or some slight variant of these words) (Gen 1:28). As I pointed out in the previous chapter, many people in the West came to interpret the words of the book of Genesis as a mandate to exploit the plants, the animals and the earth itself.

However, within the past generation we have learned to interpret these words in a more respectful and benign manner. We now understand them to mean that God has given us responsibility for the care of the earth and its creatures. There is a verse in one of the psalms which in previous English versions was translated as: 'You have given man dominion ... putting all things under his feet' (Ps 8:7). In the light of our new understanding of the need for an ecological spirituality, a more appropriate translation is: 'You entrust us with the works of your hands, inviting us to care for all of creation.'

What is required is not an exploitative attitude but what we may call 'a down-to-earth wisdom'. Indeed, there is a beautiful passage in the Book of Wisdom which may be translated as follows:

> God of our ancestors, God of mercy, you have made the whole of creation by your Word. In your power you have given us responsibility for the creation and for all the creatures you have made. ... Give us the wisdom who sits by your throne ... Wisdom who knows your works and was present when you made the world. Send her forth ... so that she may be with us and work with us ... for she knows and understands all things and will guide us gently, safely and prudently in all that we do. *(Wis 9:1-17)*

This passage suggests that a crucial part of an authentic spirituality is a practical ecological wisdom – one which will guide us in making prudent choices about how to care for the earth. In this chapter I shall first offer a variety of suggestions about what each of us can do as individuals. Then I shall go on to look at some of the big issues which can only be resolved at governmental and international level.

Global Warming and our Lifestyle
Nowadays, the topic of global warming is on everybody's lips. But most of the talk is about the kind of action that should be taken by others – by governments, or the United Nations, or multinational companies. This is understandable because at first sight the problem seems to be one that is too big for any one of us to tackle. However, it is becoming increasingly clear that there are significant steps that can be taken by individuals. And it is vitally important that a whole lot of individuals like ourselves should make changes in our way of living. We can then hope that this will lead to a build-up of commitment and of pressure on governments and companies to a point where they are compelled to take the major corrective action that is required.

There are many fairly small actions we can do without too much difficulty. Each of these is important because it contributes in some degree to lessening the problem. Equally important is the fact that doing them will keep the problem in the forefront of our minds. This means that we will be on the lookout for other actions we can take. It means also that we will be giving good example to others.

Engaging in such relatively minor actions day by day may even have the effect of broadening the deep desire of our hearts to a point where we devote ourselves to practical ecological commitment and campaign to convince others of its importance. Then those of us who are in a position to do so will feel confident in speaking out on the urgency of the issue of global warming, rather than remaining silent because of our own inaction and sense of helplessness or guilt. At the risk of being accused of 'preaching at people', I venture now to list a variety of practical ways in which we can live in a way that puts less demands on the environment.

Many of us drive cars. We need to ask ourselves whether we could use public transport more frequently for our longer journeys and whether we could walk or use a bicycle for shorter distances. I need hardly say that we should disapprove of the use of gas-guzzling SUVs. We might take the risk of discouraging our friends from buying these monsters.

One of the simplest actions each of us can take is simply to use less water – especially hot water. Quite frequently people run the hot tap for three minutes just to get enough hot water to rinse a cup or a plate. This means that large amounts of hot water are being drawn out of the tank and left sitting in the many yards of piping between the tank and the tap. It would be far more eco-friendly to have a water-heating device very close to the tap, or else to wash a lot of cups and plates at the same time. And when washing objects or ourselves we may not need to run the taps at full force.

From the point of view of our spirituality, it is important that we find ways of ensuring that our ecological action and campaigning is satisfying and enjoyable. It should not be a great burden which weighs us down with guilt – and we must also ensure that we do not come across to our friends and colleagues as trying to put them on a guilt-trip.

Our Carbon Footprint

A phrase that has come into use quite recently is 'our carbon footprint', meaning the extent to which each one of us personally contributes to the amount of carbon in the atmosphere and therefore to global warming. Air travel is one of the major ways in which we increase our carbon footprint – because aeroplanes spew out a huge amount of carbon, and they also produce other by-products which are even more damaging than carbon. Over the past twenty years, with the development of no-frills low-cost airlines, there has been an enormous increase in air travel. Even the rapid rise in the price of aero-fuel has not yet led to a significant drop in the amount of plane journeys. We need to ask ourselves whether we could perhaps take our holidays nearer home – and, in doing so, whether we can make sure that such holidays are truly refreshing, enjoyable, and nourishing for body and spirit.

What about our houses: how well insulated are they? Could we install more insulation and ensure that drafts are eliminated? We should also check to see whether our house has a modern efficient boiler and whether the hot water cylinder is lagged abundantly. Have we taken sufficient account of the new or improved technologies such as solar panels and wind-powered generators? Not so long ago these were associated mainly with 'far out' enthusiasts, but now they are becoming mainstream.

Much of the food we eat, and the wine we may occasionally drink, comes from far-off parts of the world. Low-priced oil has led us in the Western world to see other continents as our orchards and farms, the places where our fruit and much of our food and drink is produced. It has been calculated that the shipping of these goods from distant lands adds significantly to global warming.

It seems likely that in the not-too-distant future, when global warming has increased and when oil is running out and has become far more expensive than at present, we shall have to go back to relying more on local food, drink, and other products. Would it be possible for us to begin this process at the present time? A very practical initiative would be to grow most of our own vegetables, as many families did in the past. By doing so we would be reminding ourselves of the urgency of the global warming issue, living closer to the earth, and modelling a more ecological lifestyle for others.

Perhaps the most important thing we can all do to save our planet for the future is to scale down what we see as our needs. Most of us survived quite well thirty or forty years ago, living a much simpler life, perhaps a life closer to the earth. Those of us who, like myself, lived as children in rural areas in the 1930s and 1940s may recall that at that time ninety percent or our food was locally produced. We now have the possibility of going back to some extent to that situation by supporting the local farmer markets which are becoming more common.

All of these changes of lifestyle can be made for purely practical reasons, with little or no advertence to any spirituality. But they can also be undertaken as a way of embodying our spirituality in practice. Our care for the environment can be a means of showing our gratitude for the nourishment of spirit which it provides. It is important that we make these practical activities an integral part of our ecological spirituality. People who are seeking to live out their Christian faith very consciously may find it helpful, as they cut down the wasteful use of resources and scale down their needs, to reflect on the simple life lived by Jesus.

Food
There are major issues around the kind of food eaten today by most people in the West, as well as by an increasing number of people in developing countries. One important issue has to do with health. A recent official government report in the UK[1] estimates that the failure to follow nutritional guidelines results in 70,000 premature deaths each year in that country. Furthermore, bad eating habits cause a huge amount of health problems, and the treatment of these illnesses imposes a major burden on the economy. In the world as a whole it is estimated that there are now 300 million obese people. This contrasts sharply with the 800 million who are left hungry due to poverty and lack of access to food.

A second major issue concerns the environment. In the West, at present, most of our food comes to us through agribusiness companies. The way in which this food is produced and packaged uses very large amounts of energy, and generates huge amounts of waste. Food production puts enormous demands on water supplies – to such an extent that in many areas of the world the demand is no longer sustainable. Furthermore, the production and consumption of food is responsible for 18% of the greenhouse gases emitted in some Western countries.

Food prices have risen very sharply within the past year. For a variety of reasons, it is likely that they will continue to rise. One reason is the growing shortage of energy supplies and of clean water. Another is the recent switch from the production of food to bio-fuels. A third reason is that the population of the world is still growing quite quickly. A further reason is that a small number of major agribusiness companies now control a

1.www.cabinetoffice.gov.uk/~/media/assets/www.cabinetoffice. gov.uk/strategy/food/food_matters%20pdf.ashx

very large segment of the market; they are making huge profits at the expense of consumers and small-scale farmers. Finally, the rapidly growing middle classes in Asia are now eating far more meat – and production of meat demands several times as much use of land and water, and produces far more greenhouse gases, than the corresponding amount of food from grains or vegetables.

Rising food prices have a major impact on the poorest people. Very wealthy people in the West spend just 7% of their income on food. The corresponding figure for the poor in developing countries is between 50% and 80%. So the increase in food prices is a far more serious problem for these poor people.

Two conclusions emerge from all this. The first is that there is an urgent need for a major change in the way food is produced and packaged. The second conclusion is that for reasons of health and of justice, as well as for environmental reasons, many of us need to make a big change in the kind of foods we buy and eat. It would be good for ourselves and good for the world, especially for the poorest people, if we, the better-off people of the world, consumed less meat – and in many cases if we simply did not eat so much. Our spirituality needs to be broad enough to include recognising and acting on this conclusion.

Political Action as part of Ecological Spirituality

So far I have been looking at practical ways in which each of us as individuals can live out an ecological spirituality. But this is only one part of the story. The reality today is that much of the active side of our ecological spirituality must take a political shape – by campaigning on key issues and lobbying our governments on them. This is because only governments and intergovernmental agencies are in a position to take effective action to control much of the damage that is being done to the environment.

At the national level, it is easy to list the kind of measures that are required, but far harder to have them implemented. There is need for a switch in priority from road-building to the development of low-cost efficient public transport systems. Another obvious necessity is the introduction of a carbon tax which is proportionate to the amount of fossil fuel used by each company and each individual. Governments need to insist on recycling and to impose heavy sanctions on those who generate unnecessary waste. They need to ensure that there is no waste of water, either in the pipes which carry the water to houses or in the households themselves. It is also important that they encourage organic farming – perhaps through subsidies or through the imposition of taxes on pesticides and damaging fertilisers.

Moving from the national level to the international level, one of the most urgent issues is the protection of the remaining equatorial forests of Brazil, Indonesia, and other countries. Another obvious example is the conservation of the fish stocks of the oceans which are being rapidly depleted. There is urgent need for intergovernmental agreements, under the auspices of the United Nations, to put an end to over-fishing. Similarly, we need universally binding covenants to ensure that toxic wastes are not dumped at sea or in poor countries. The build-up of nuclear waste is an issue which needs to be addressed. At present, many countries are leaving a poisonous legacy to future generations.

Perhaps even more urgent – and more difficult – is the need for binding agreements to reduce the amount of carbon that is spewed out into the atmosphere both by the industrialised countries of the West and by countries like China and India which are industrialising so rapidly at present. Related to this is the need to make sure that 'carbon credit schemes', if they are used at all, are realistic and efficient. At present many of them seem to be used as ways in which industrialised countries can avoid facing up to difficult decisions about reducing the amount of carbon they produce.[2]

How can we work to bring about these changes in national policies and the introduction and enforcement of the kind of international covenants which I have mentioned? The only way in which it can happen is by very large numbers of people putting

2. On all of these issues one of the most prolific and effective campaigners is Sean McDonagh. See, for instance, *Dying for Water*, Dublin: Veritas, 2003; *The Death of Life: Extinction Is Forever*, Dublin: Columba Press, 2004; *Climate Change: the Challenge to All of Us*, Dublin: Columba Press, 2006. A particularly trenchant critic of present ecological practices is George Monbiot in *Bring on the Apocalypse*, London: Atlantic Books, 2008, pp 29-63. See also Alastair McIntosh, *Hell and High Water: Climate Change, Hope and the Human Condition*, Edinburgh: Birlinn, 2008.

sustained pressure on their governments to take a lead in getting them implemented. In practice, this means organising or supporting 'green' organisations or movements. Some people will do this by playing an active role in Green political parties. Others may find it preferable or more effective to put pressure on their traditional political parties to ensure that they adopt 'green' policies.

We should not be ashamed to bring spirituality into the campaign, linking it with practical economic arguments for decisive action. There is sound evidence that the conjunction of spiritual and well-grounded ecological arguments can produce results. A few years ago there were plans to begin mining for gold on the side of Croagh Patrick, the most sacred mountain in Ireland. Work on the project was already well under way when an unusual alliance emerged to oppose it. The alliance brought together nature enthusiasts who were determined to preserve this pristine landscape, local farmers and others who feared that the land and water would be polluted by the use of poisonous chemicals in the mining process, and spiritually-minded people who were outraged at the prospect of the desecration of the holy mountain. The politicians who had previously encouraged the mining operation quickly changed their minds and the mining project was abandoned.

Genetic Modification
The issue of genetic modification has recently become very urgent. It is one where people committed to an ecological spirituality need to demand firm action at national and international level.

From very early times we humans have made changes in the world around us. Trees have been cut down to make fields and gardens. Land has been drained or irrigated or terraced to ensure more productive crops. Domestic animals have been bred to upgrade the quantity and quality of meat and milk they produce. All of these interventions in nature can be seen as ways in which we humans are privileged to be co-creators with God by shaping the world and even guiding the process of evolution.

A particularly important way in which humans can co-operate with God in the work of creation is through scientific research, because it enables us to discover and develop more effective ways of promoting human welfare and the enhancement of the environment. In recent times there has been rapid development in the physical, chemical, and biological sciences. This has led to a significant rise in the number and frequency of technological breakthroughs. This, in turn, has brought about an enormous increase in our power to control and change both ourselves and our environment. Now, for the first time, we humans have the ability to exercise our co-creative powers in a truly radical way. This is a great spiritual privilege. But it is also a fundamental spiritual challenge. For we can misuse our power over nature and use it to damage or even destroy ourselves and our world.

One of the most radical ways in which our power over nature can be used is by changing the genetic makeup of plants, of animals, and even of humans. Here I shall focus on the issue of the modification of the genes of plants, since it is a particularly pressing issue at this time. Unfortunately, much of the scientific research on genetic modification which is taking place today is not being carried out by scientists engaged in a disinterested search for truth, or in a disinterested attempt to improve human welfare. Instead it is sponsored either directly or indirectly by multinational companies involved in agri-business. Its ultimate purpose is to enable the companies who fund it to make greater profits – and it is all too easy for this to undermine the objectivity of the research.

We can no longer be sure that the reported results accurately reflect the outcome of the research. Time after time we hear of situations where reports on research have been doctored or edited to eliminate or play down results which would cast doubt on the value of new products, and on the benefits which they are supposed to bring. Harmful side-effects or long-term consequences are concealed, or there is a failure to take account of the effects which the applications of the research may have in the wider society. Furthermore, conscientious scientists are likely to run into difficulties if they dare to express doubts about the value of the research or about ways in which it may be used.

The large agribusiness companies are devoting huge resources to the development of genetically modified seeds and particularly of seeds using what has come to be called 'terminator technology'. Terminator seeds are deliberately designed in a way that causes the next generation of seeds to be sterile. This means that no crop can be produced from the seeds of plants grown from the terminator seeds. So farmers have to buy new seeds each year instead of using some of the seeds of each year's crop to grow the plants of the following year.

Half of the farmers of the world are poor. They have survived up to now by carrying seeds over from one year to the next and by sharing seeds with each other. The use of genetically modified seeds is already undermining this system. Furthermore, their use does enormous damage to the environment. This is because, at the present time, the use of genetically modified seeds is just one part of a whole system of agriculture which is dependent on the use of poisonous herbicides and large amounts of chemical fertilisers which degrade the whole ecosystem.

The widespread use of terminator technology would take this process a step further. It would effectively put a complete end to the traditional system of carrying over seeds from one harvest to the next. Consequently, it would leave farmers entirely at the mercy of the transnational agribusiness companies.

There is so much alarm and protest about the effects of terminator technology that at present there is a moratorium on its use. But the companies which have developed it are trying to get around the ban on its use by developing variants using what is called T-GURT. This allows the sterility of the seed to be reversed – but only through the use of a chemical which the farmer has to buy from the company. These seeds have been dubbed 'zombie seeds' by those who oppose them.

Anybody who is trying to live out a genuine ecological spirituality cannot remain neutral in the face of terminator technology. We are obliged to judge its use to be morally unacceptable for a variety of reasons. First of all, it has the effect of lessening bio-diversity. It brings about a radical reduction in variety in the strains of rice, maize, wheat and other food crops; and the few remaining strains could be wiped out by some virulent disease. This would leave millions of people open to the possibility of famine or food shortage. Furthermore, it is a technology which has not yet been adequately and objectively tested as regards its long-term consequences. It could have effects which are damaging both to the environment and to future generations of people.

A further moral objection to terminator technology and to genetic engineering in general is that it increases the extent to which the global market or the local market in seeds is controlled by a small group of companies. This means that the producers and consumers are left largely at the mercy of these companies. It enables a small number of corporations to gain a monopoly of some significant part of the environment. So it lessens the extent to which the environment and control of the environment is shared by all. In this way it leads to a widening of the gap between the rich and the poor, the powerful and those who are disempowered. In the light of these moral considerations it is important that ecologically committed people continue to put pressure on their governments to impose strict controls on research into genetic modification and to strengthen and make permanent the moratorium on all forms of terminator technology.

A Role for Churches and Religious Communities

Over the past generation the World Council of Churches and many of its member churches have taken a lead role in working for ecological responsibility. Furthermore, they have recognised the close link between the environmental question and the issue of justice in the world. This is summed up in their commitment to 'Justice, Peace, and the Integrity of Creation' (JPIC).

During the papacy of John Paul II the Catholic Church seemed rather reluctant to bring the issue of ecological responsibility to the forefront of its moral agenda. One of the strengths of John Paul's approach to morality was his strong emphasis on being fully human. Unfortunately, there was a perhaps unintended side-effect of this approach: it led the pope to make an unduly sharp contrast between humans and the rest of nature – and caused him to play down the ecological agenda. Pope Benedict has moved to correct this imbalance by repeatedly making powerful statements about the need to protect the environment.[3]

3. e.g. his address to some 400 priests of the diocese of Bolzano-Bressanone, August 6, 2008.

In some religious circles there is a fear that those who adopt an ecological spirituality will take on the New Age idea of going back to the nature religions of the past – a return to paganism. It seems to me that the best way to avoid this danger is for Christians to develop a spirituality which combines orthodox belief with respect for the sacredness of the created world. It is particularly important that we Christians should not allow environmental concern to be associated mainly with a secularist agenda. Instead we should play a leading role in developing an ecological spirituality in both its contemplative and its active aspects.

Religious congregations and missionary societies ought to be to the forefront on this issue – as they are already on issues of justice at the national and international levels. Would it be helpful for them to set up one or more 'ecology desks' corresponding to the 'justice desks' which serve them so well in their individual organisations and in the agencies where they work together? On the whole, I am inclined to think that it would be better not to do so. It would be preferable to extend the mandate of the 'justice desk' so that it includes – and gives a prominent place to – an active and contemplative ecological spirituality. I hope that the close links between justice and ecology will become more evident in Chapter 15 which is devoted to a spirituality of social justice.

CHAPTER FOURTEEN

A Spirituality of Human Rights

As I pointed out in the Introduction, there has been a tendency in recent years to give an account of spirituality very much in terms of meditative techniques leading to personal tranquillity. Without playing down this aspect, I have been trying to offer a more rounded and comprehensive account. I want to emphasise the fact that morality is a key element in spirituality. In the case of ecological spirituality, I hope that the previous two chapters have shown the close connection between its two aspects – the contemplative aspect in which we focused on how contact with the earth can bring personal serenity by nourishing the human spirit, and the more active moral aspect which focuses on our obligation to care for the earth.

In the present chapter I move on to outline a spirituality of human rights. At first sight it might seem more appropriate to describe human rights in terms of duty or even of law, rather than linking rights to spirituality. But the title of this book is 'Spirituality, Our Deepest Heart's Desire' and it is obvious that there are millions of people all over the world whose deep heart's desire is to bring about a world where fundamental human rights are respected. Indeed, many of them have put their lives or their freedom on the line in defence of human rights, and quite a lot of people have died in this cause. Furthermore, many good people who might not claim that the defence of human rights is the deepest desire of their hearts, nevertheless feel outraged and deeply troubled at heart when they hear of gross abuses of fundamental rights. For these reasons it is necessary to include the commitment to human rights as an important aspect of a fully rounded spirituality.

The development of a spirituality of human rights involves first of all getting to know what human rights are considered to be fundamental, and what progress has been made so far in codifying rights and making the observance of human rights a matter of legitimate international concern. It also involves becoming more aware of when and how this new emphasis on human rights emerged, exploring some of its strengths and weaknesses, and seeing how it compares with an older 'natural law' approach. I shall devote most of the present chapter to these questions, because the knowledge of many people about human rights is quite vague and inadequate.

Later in this chapter I shall move on to consider an aspect of the spirituality of rights which is of more immediate concern for the purpose of this book. It is the development in one's everyday life of a personal attitude of deep respect for the rights of others. This, in turn, will lead me on to consider the fostering of a culture of respect for fundamental human rights, at local, national, and international levels.

Declarations, Covenants and Conventions
Much of the moral and political progress which has taken place in recent decades has come through the codification of a wide variety of human rights, and the embodiment of these rights in a series of international agreements which make the observance of these rights by states a matter of legitimate concern to the international community as a whole. Not all of these rights are respected in practice by the governments which have signed up to them. Nevertheless, the formal commitment which a large number of governments have entered into to observe these rights marks a real advance in human civilisation.

The adoption by the United Nations General Assembly in 1948 of 'The Universal Declaration of Human Rights' was what we might call 'the foundational event' in this process. This declaration set out a range of major civil and political rights, including the following:

- The right to life, liberty and security of person and the right not to be held in slavery or servitude.
- The right not to be subjected to torture or to cruel, inhuman or degrading treatment or punishment.
- The right not to be subjected to arbitrary arrest, detention or exile.
- The right to freedom of movement and residence within the

borders of each state and the right to leave one's country and to return to it.

- The right to seek and to enjoy in other countries asylum from persecution.
- The right to freedom of peaceful assembly and association.
- The right to take part in the government of one's country, directly or through freely chosen representatives.
- The right to own property alone and in association with others.
- The right to freedom of thought, conscience and religion and to manifest one's religion or belief in teaching, practice, worship and observance.

The *Universal Declaration of Human Rights* went on to enumerate a variety of economic, social and cultural rights. These included the following:

- The right to work, to free choice of employment, to just and favourable conditions of work and to protection against unemployment.
- The right to equal pay for equal work.
- The right of workers to just and favourable remuneration ensuring for themselves and their families an existence worthy of human dignity, and supplemented, if necessary, by other means of social protection.
- The right to form and to join trade unions.
- The right to rest and leisure, including reasonable limitation of working hours and periodic holidays with pay.
- The right to a standard of living adequate for the health and well-being of oneself and of one's family, including food, clothing, housing and medical care and necessary social services.
- The right to security in the event of unemployment, sickness, disability, widowhood, old age or other lack of livelihood in circumstances beyond one's control.
- The entitlement of mothers and children to special care and assistance.
- The right to free education, at least in the elementary and fundamental stages.

The Universal Declaration was not legally binding, but it led on to a strong movement to have its provisions given binding force through an international treaty which would be ratified by the individual states which are members of the United Nations. There was general acceptance, at least in principle, that the civil and political rights could be given a binding legal status. But there were serious difficulties in relation to the economic and social rights. Governments of poorer countries knew that, so long as their countries remained poor, they simply could not afford to implement some of these rights.

Furthermore, many governments, particularly in Western countries, felt that it was a mistake to give economic and social rights a legal status. Their objection was not merely because they felt the list was unrealistic. Their reluctance also had a more ideological basis: according to capitalist theory, economic matters should mainly be left to the market. This unwillingness to legislate on economic affairs led to a long delay in getting the rights named in the 'Universal Declaration' carried through into binding international agreements and into the domestic legislation of countries.

Eventually, two distinct 'covenants' or international treaties were agreed on in 1966. The first of these was the 'International Covenant on Civil and Political Rights'. By 1976 a sufficient number of the member countries of the UN had ratified it, so that it came into force in that year. The second covenant was the 'International Covenant on Economic, Social and Cultural Rights'. This latter treaty is much weaker than the one on civil and political rights. It only commits each of the 155 states which have signed and ratified it 'to take steps ... to the maximum of its available resources, with a view to achieving progressively the full realisation of the rights recognised in the present Covenant by all appropriate means ...' It is clear that the phrases 'to take steps' and 'achieving progressively' can be used as an excuse for failures by a country to implement the provisions of the treaty fully. Another more practical source of weakness of this second treaty is that it was never ratified by the US Senate, even though President Jimmy Carter of the USA had signed it.

In recent years, under the auspices of the United Nations, a further wide variety of fundamental human rights have come to be enumerated and spelled out in legislation at the international

level. These are contained in a series of 'conventions'. For instance, there is a convention concerned with the elimination of
all forms of racial discrimination, which came into force in 1969,
and one dealing with the elimination of all forms of discrimination against women, which came into force in 1981. Then there
is the 'Convention against Torture' which was adopted in 1984,
and the 'Convention on the Rights of the Child', which was
adopted in 1989. The rights of people who are 'trafficked' (for
sexual or other forms of slavery or exploitation) are protected
through a specific protocol added to the United Nations
'Convention against Transnational Organized Crime'. At present, many countries all over the world are enacting legislation
which is designed to eliminate the horror of the trafficking of
people.[1]

Historical Background
Although there is widespread agreement about most of these
fundamental human rights, there is a wide divergence of opinion when it comes to identifying the basis for such rights. It
seems to be a matter of historical fact that the recent attempts to
spell out specific human rights took place largely under the influence of Western philosophical thought. The Judeo-Christian
tradition has been a constant background influence in Western
philosophy, even though quite a lot of the theory on human
rights has developed within a liberal and humanist tradition
which has sought to find a non-religious basis for human rights.

Although the Western liberal tradition has been the dominant force in the codifying of human rights in our time, it is worth
noting that the rights of women, of children and of slaves were
specified far earlier in the 'Code of Hammurabi', which was developed in Mesopotamia more than three-and-a-half thousand
years ago. Various elements of human rights thinking can also
be found in the ancient Indian scriptures, in the work of
Confucius in China, and in the Brehon Laws of ancient Ireland,
as well as in the bible and the Qur'an.

Historically, there have been two major approaches to finding a basis for ensuring that people live with respect for each

1. See, for instance, www.actionagainsttrafficking.org and the links on
that website.

other. The first is the 'natural law' approach which derives largely from Aristotle and was developed by theologians and philosophers in the Middle Ages and up to more recent times; it put a major emphasis on 'the common good'. A rather different approach, centred on 'rights', has come to be seen by many modern thinkers as an alternative to the 'natural law' approach. This 'rights' approach goes back to the British philosopher John Locke and was given a strong emphasis in the Constitution of the USA and its various amendments. In more recent times, fundamental human rights have had a central role in jurisprudence and in a good deal of moral philosophy.

Up to quite recently Catholic Church leaders and theologians, as well as many in the Anglican tradition, tended to look with some suspicion or even hostility on the idea of making human rights a key feature of morality. Conversely, those who emphasised human rights were inclined to reject or denigrate the whole notion of 'natural law'. It was unfortunate and unnecessary that such a sharp opposition was made between the two approaches.

Those on either side of this opposition could point to weaknesses on the other side. Many of the defenders of the rights approach naïvely assumed that such rights are self-evident. This left them open to the objection that they had no way of resolving situations where there was an apparent clash of rights. On the other hand, the proponents of the natural law approach tended to understand natural law in an unduly mechanistic way – as though each creature and object in the world comes with its own built-in set of easily readable and unchanging rules. A more flexible and holistic understanding of natural law fits quite comfortably with an approach to morality which emphasises fundamental human rights but does not assume that they are self-evident.

The More Recent Catholic Approach
Because of the suspicion of church leaders of the human rights approach to morality, it was only in relatively recent times that Catholic social teaching began to refer to human rights in favourable terms. Pope John XXIII in his 1963 encyclical letter *Pacem in Terris* (Peace in the World) played a notable part in this

shift. Since that time Catholic Church authorities have put more and more emphasis on the importance of respect for human rights.

Recent pronouncements of Catholic Church authorities have insisted that individuals and governments must respect the right to life, to freedom of conscience and religion, to security, to work, to a family income, to the ownership of property, and to an education, as well as the right to have one's culture respected. They have also insisted on the right not to be discriminated against on the basis of gender, race, wealth, or social status. According to Christian teaching, prejudices such as racism, homophobia and sexism are to be challenged.

However, the social teaching of the Catholic Church does not just list a whole series of self-evident or self-justifying rights. It begins rather with the fundamental principle that every human person is made in the image of God and therefore has an inherent dignity which must be respected by others. This means that human dignity is seen as the source or basis, under God, for fundamental human rights. Human rights are not seen as self-justifying; they derive rather from the person's God-given dignity. Furthermore, the highlighting of human rights has been integrated into other key principles of Catholic social teaching: a strong emphasis on the common good, on human solidarity, and on participation, as well as on the principle of subsidiarity, and on a preferential option for the poor. More recently, care for the environment has also been given prominence.[2]

We Christians have to acknowledge that much of what we now accept as Christian social teaching on human rights is drawn from the thinking of non-Christian – sometimes anti-Christian – philosophers and political thinkers and activists. For example, much of the church's recent thinking and teaching on democracy, human rights, ecology, and the role of women was first worked out by people who were not Christians. Sadly, many of these ideas were strongly condemned by church leaders in the past. It was only slowly and reluctantly that the church authorities came to accept the importance of such ideas. There is

2. I have treated this topic in more detail in a chapter entitled 'An Introduction to Catholic Social Teaching', pp 192-201 of Anne Hession and Patricia Kieran (editors), *Exploring Theology: Making Sense of the Catholic Tradition,* Dublin: Veritas, 2007.

a lesson to be learned here: in the future, church leaders should be less rigid in holding on to outdated ideas. They ought to be more open to new developments and issues – for instance, in relation to cultural diversity and globalisation.

Strengths and Weaknesses of Human Rights

Probably the greatest strength of an approach to spirituality centred on human rights is that it touches a deep chord in people of today's world. Every day we hear of dreadful abuses of human rights – for instance, torture of prisoners, sexual abuse of children, and the flouting of democracy by tyrannical governments. One does not have to be a philosopher, theologian or legal theorist to be outraged by such abuses. Using traditional language, one might say this kind of behaviour 'cries out to heaven for vengeance'. People empathise with those whose fundamental rights are denied – perhaps because they can easily imagine themselves suffering the same indignities.

One of the weaknesses of an approach to morality based on human rights is that it tends to put the main emphasis on the rights of individuals. Undoubtedly, some rights, such as the right not to be tortured, are so inalienable that they can never be abrogated. But there are other individual rights which have to be seen in the context of the common good of whole communities – and it is not always easy for people to accept that limitation. Indeed some of the prominence given to personal rights can at times reinforce the excessive individualism which is a feature of the Western world: people may be so focused on their own rights that they are insensitive to the rights of others and to the common good.

There is also a danger that an approach based on human rights may over-state the difference between humans and the rest of the natural world. This can lead to an insensitivity and an exploitative attitude towards the non-human creatures with whom we share this world.

A Wider Context

It is particularly important to situate both human rights and natural law against the background of an ecological vision. In this vision we see the earth as an incredibly complex interlocking and self-sustaining but fragile system. This earth system is itself an integral part of the immensely larger system which is the universe or the cosmos.

We humans are not masters of our own destiny with a mandate to exploit the earth as we will. We are dependent for our existence from moment to moment on the proper working of innumerable physical, chemical, biological and psychological systems of which we have, as yet, quite limited understanding and over most of which we have very inadequate control. Consequently, it is only quite tentatively and at our peril that we can venture to act in ways which might disrupt these systems.

Against this background, human rights must be seen in a context where we recognise that each of us is part of the wider world. They must not be based on a conception of humanity which assumes that humans are quite different from the rest of creation.[3] It does not make sense to treat fundamental human rights as though they were simply self-evident or self-justifying.

Similarly, 'natural law' has to be seen not just as the 'book of rules' of particular categories of creatures. We need to see it first of all as an obligation to respect the working of the system as a whole. This requires that one has some understanding of the multifaceted inter-relationships of its different parts. Furthermore, the older static conception of natural law must yield to one which takes very seriously the process of evolution which is the most significant feature of the natural world.

Respect

Having listed various human rights and looked at the historical background, I am now moving on to the second key element in a spirituality of rights. This is the importance of developing in our day-to-day life a personal attitude of deep respect for the rights

---

3. A striking example of the continuity between humans and animals is the recent scientific evidence that some of the higher animals have the ability to empathise with others – they feel concern when they see others in pain and they modify their behaviour accordingly, in somewhat the same way as humans do. The two foundational pillars of our human morality are, firstly, our rational powers, which are uniquely human, and, secondly, our capacity for empathy with others, which may be seen as a development and refinement of an ability which we share with animals.

of others and how to live this out in our spirituality. This is central to the purpose of this book.

I begin by noting that when dealing with this aspect of a spirituality of rights we are concerned not just with legal obligations but primarily with psychological attitudes. Everything hinges on the key word 'respect'. When people speak or write about 'respecting human rights', this is usually taken in a *legal* context. So 'respecting' comes to mean 'not interfering with'. Such a legal approach is, of course, essential. But 'not interfering with' is a negative conception which is only a basic minimum of what is involved in respect. An authentic spirituality of human rights requires that we go much further.

Should we not see the word 'respect' as more or less equivalent to 'reverence'? Instead of just seeing others as people whom we should not hurt or obstruct, our spirituality invites us to empathise with them, to be aware of their fragility and vulnerability. This can lead us to reverence them, to love them, and even to treasure them. At its best, our spirituality can inspire us to treat others with great *tenderness*. Ideally we should find ourselves looking at each person as a sacred being, as a mystery before whom we at times feel like bowing in awe and veneration.

In practice, this means nurturing the empathetic aspect of ourselves, so that increasingly we begin 'to walk in the other person's shoes'. This involves being so much in tune with the feelings of others that we become fully sensitive to their needs. The result is that we are spontaneously inclined to respect their rights and the rights of the community.

For most of us, this requires a quite radical conversion. One aspect of it is a conversion at the moral level, where we commit ourselves unreservedly to 'loving our neighbour as ourselves'. But there is also another aspect, namely, an affective conversion. This means having our spontaneous feelings come into line with our moral commitment.[4]

As I said in the Introduction, this is not strictly a 'how to' book, so I am not dealing here with techniques for bringing about this affective conversion. I need only say that for some people it may require quite a lot of personal development work. It may even necessitate some counselling or therapy in order to

4. Cf footnote 1 on p 46 above.

heal the wounds of the past. Furthermore, those whose work involves dealing with others at a deep personal level will find it helpful, even essential, to have regular supervision of their work.

Fostering a Culture of Respect

The third element in a spirituality of human rights is the fostering of a culture of respect for fundamental rights at all levels – local, national, and international. For much of the time this may involve acting in a counter-cultural way, since individualism and an exploitative attitude are prominent features in the culture of today's world.

A faulty conception of human development has tended to give a certain legitimacy to the insensitive and abusive attitudes which are an intrinsic part of human sinfulness. Theories of economic development encouraged people to *exploit* the natural resources which were available to them – oil, minerals, timber, and land. The resultant insensitivity to nature fostered an attitude of *using* things and people, in the sense of taking advantage of them. This involved a deep-seated disrespect for anything or anybody that stood in the way of so-called development. The result has been that the word 'exploit' has been given a positive meaning which, for much of the time, seems to replace its negative connotation.

Those who live out an authentic spirituality of human rights pose a radical challenge to this attitude. Needless to say, the primary way in which they do so is by the pattern of their own lives as individuals and in communities. It is their personal witness to the values of respect, reverence, and sensitivity that makes them effective agents of challenge and change.

However, though that is vitally important, the people committed to a spirituality of rights know that it is not sufficient. They also feel called to play an active role in educating public opinion on emerging human rights issues. They must also engage in active dialogue with politicians and governments at the national level. In recent years a number of agencies representing religious groups have been accredited to the United Nations. The people who staff these agencies have engaged in fruitful dialogue with those deeply committed diplomats who have taken on the task of negotiating international treaties in relation to human rights. It is worth noting that most of these international treaties, which were negotiated by diplomats and ultimately spelled out by legal experts, came as a result of much lobbying and campaigning by committed 'amateurs'. On the other hand, there were situations where it was left to the diplomats to work out a compromise when the different groups of campaigners could not agree with each other.

Protests and Campaigns

There are times when a spirituality of human rights involves protesting against abuses, both at home and abroad. In many situations the protest is costly and risky. It involves putting the abusers on the defensive. It is a very short step from defensiveness to aggression – especially when the challenge is being posed to powerful people or tyrannical regimes. In today's world, people are being martyred every day because of their devotion to the cause of human rights. Their courage and fortitude is an inspiration and source of energy to those of us who have to face far less serious penalties – perhaps the loss of a desired promotion, or just the discomfort of being criticised for being disloyal, or being labelled as cranks.

There is only a limited amount anybody can achieve by acting alone. A fully effective spirituality of human rights has to be lived out by a community of people. Ideally, it should be a local community, one which links up with other local communities in the same country and in the wider world. However, the reality today is that we may often have to settle for what might be called 'a virtual community' – a widely scattered group of like-minded people linked together by email or on the web.

Such groups have had some notable successes in campaigning for human rights and offering support to those who find themselves 'on the cutting edge' of the struggle. For much of the time these back-up campaigners may do so by working through Amnesty International or other agencies whose primary aim is the protection and fostering of human rights. Occasionally they may become involved in once-off letter-writing campaigns, or in boycotts, marches or other public protests.

Campaigning for human rights is often an exciting activity,

but also a demanding and stressful one. Consequently, it can easily happen that campaigners become so caught up in the struggle that they begin to lose touch with that deep place within themselves where their spirituality is nurtured. For this reason it is important that they remember that the struggle for human rights is only one part of a fully rounded spirituality. They may need, at times, to shift their focus. They may perhaps even need to take some 'time out' to replenish their energies and allow themselves to be touched more deeply and in different ways by the Spirit whose power is the heartbeat of any authentic spirituality.

CHAPTER FIFTEEN

A Spirituality of Social Justice

Once again I note the danger of reducing spirituality to just one of its two major dimensions – putting all the focus on the personal and inward-looking aspect, to the neglect of the outward-looking aspect which deals with how we humans live together in a peaceful and equitable society. In the workshops which I conduct on spirituality, many of the participants give a rather low priority to issues of social justice. Indeed, for many people today spirituality seems to exist in a different sphere from their concern about the major injustices which mar our world.

In the chapters on ecology and on rights I attempted to remedy this imbalance by showing the need for an integral spirituality which takes account of both dimensions. In this chapter I hope to carry this further by describing how major social injustices emerge. This will lead on to noting how the science of economics is misused to justify and reinforce this injustice. I shall leave over to the following chapter an account of how mainstream economics can be challenged by a spirituality based on the bible.

Traditional Society
In traditional societies each local area is generally self-sufficient in the production of food. Not merely each area, but even most families can manage to meet their own needs as regards staple foods. For the most part, what is consumed locally is produced locally and *vice versa*.

If the people are hunter-gatherers, they have to be so spread out that each family group has only occasional contact with other families. In that situation there is little need for political authorities; and so there is only limited scope for major social injustice.

Once people begin to plant crops and domesticate animals they tend to live more closely together. Then there is need for an organised system to ensure the harmony and welfare of the local people. In tribal societies, decisions are usually taken by some kind of local council. This council will probably consist of elders, with a chief who presides over the meeting.

Decisions are usually taken on a consensus basis. They are made by local people who themselves have immediate experience of the problems they are confronting. This reduces the likelihood that there will be serious social injustice in the society.

However, there seems to be a link between the development of agriculture and the emergence of patriarchy: in the majority of such societies women have a lower status and a less privileged position than men. The council of elders is generally composed of men, so one might suspect that the interests of women are not adequately represented there. Nevertheless, in many tribal societies women have their own organisations to safeguard their welfare.

In contrast to modern society there is little need for a large bureaucracy of civil servants in traditional societies, because each community is largely self-sufficient and therefore not very dependent on a centralised authority. There is need, of course, for some authority structure at a broader level than that of the village. So, there is somebody who is seen as the head of the clan or of a whole tribe. The role of this person is to foster harmony between the different village communities.

This 'higher' authority does not supplant the authority of the village councils, or reduce them to being its agents. The authority of the clan head comes more from the respect of the people than from the use of force. So, once again, there is little room here for gross social injustice.

In this situation there is no need for a large police force. Law enforcement takes place at a local level. The cohesion of the traditional society is greatly strengthened by the cultural traditions which emphasise community solidarity and respect for the wisdom of the older people. Religious beliefs also foster cohesion; and religious taboos and sanctions are used to ensure law enforcement.

The fabric of a traditional society is strong because it forms a coherent whole, a unified pattern. Societies that have survived over many generations have done so because they have various 'checks and balances' built into them, thereby ensuring a fair degree of equity and justice. It would, of course, be sheer romanticism to suggest that every traditional society is a perfect model of social justice. But the survival of traditional cultures provides us with historical evidence that social justice is a foundation for stability and peace.

Disrupting the Pattern

If serious social injustice is not generally a major element in traditional society, why is it that it so pervasive in modern society? The answer is that injustice arises through a growing internal imbalance or through outside interference – or, most commonly, through a combination of these two causes.

First of all, major social injustice can arise from within the society itself. In every society there are some individuals and groups who are willing to take advantage of others. However, in a smoothly functioning society the greed of such people and groups is held in check by curbs on their power. These curbs often prove inadequate in a rapidly changing society.

Sudden and unforeseen changes give more opportunity to unscrupulous people or groups to exploit and oppress those who are more vulnerable. In this way, social injustice develops and begins to grow out of control. There is no longer a balanced and equitable distribution of power and resources. The fabric of the society begins to be torn apart, as some groups or classes get most of the benefits while others have to carry most of the burdens.

The second major cause of social injustice is serious interference by some strong outside power. The most obvious kind of interference is a successful military invasion, followed by deliberate re-shaping of the political and economic structures of the society. Here I shall concentrate on what has happened in recent centuries. Over a period of more than four hundred years, the major Western colonial powers interfered grossly all over Africa, Australasia, and America, as well as in large parts of Asia. The colonies they set up were governed in a way that served the political and economic interests of the colonial powers.

Is this kind of colonial intrusion now a thing of the past? Perhaps not. The invasion of Iraq in 2003 by the USA has had effects similar to those brought about by colonial powers in the past. And there is a strong case for saying that the invasion was undertaken mainly to ensure that Iraq would get a government which would be subservient to Western (mainly American) interests.[1]

Interference from outside can also come in the cultural/religious sphere. Take, for instance, the introduction of Western health-care and educational systems into non-Western countries. Undoubtedly they have brought many benefits. Nevertheless we must acknowledge that Western medications and hospitals have undermined traditional healing practices. Similarly, Western-type education has seriously damaged the respect which young people have for their elders. Furthermore, insensitive Christian or Muslim missionaries have eroded the unity of the community by condemning traditional beliefs or rituals and by introducing serious divisions on matters of belief, conduct, and law.

The severest instances of social injustice arise when there is a combination of outside and inside causes. The most common way in which this happens is when the foreign power 'co-opts' a local power group, giving them an unfair advantage over others. In the past, the representatives of the European colonial powers often 'did a deal' with local chiefs, making them their agents in return for trading privileges.

Neo-Colonialism
Nowadays, a more common type of interference from outside comes at the economic level. It gives rise to what is called neo-colonialism. The powerful and wealthy countries maintain their economic dominance by insisting that weaker and developing countries open their markets to imports from abroad. The local market may be flooded with cheap products which are 'dumped' in a way that undermines local production.

This kind of economic intervention has become far more easy as a result of the policies of the International Monetary Fund (IMF) which are being used to promote the interests of its major shareholders, namely, the leading Western powers. The injustice is underpinned by trade agreements worked out under the

---

1. Cf Naomi Klein, *The Shock Doctrine*, Metropolitan Books: Holt & Co, New York, 2007, 327-340.

auspices of the World Trade Organization where small and weak countries find themselves at the mercy of the powerful nations. Furthermore, the World Bank, which was originally established to promote development in poorer countries, has been almost reduced to implementing IMF policies.

The key agents of neo-colonialism are the major transnational corporations, based mostly in 'the North'. They make use of a whole class of privileged local people – business people, bankers, economists, and politicians. These are co-opted as local agents of transnational companies and even of foreign governments. So they collude in the exploitation of the mass of their own people and in the destruction of the local environment. When their power is challenged they can rely on overt and covert support from abroad; and the arms they are given enables them to stifle the opposition.

The effect is that the 'independence' of these countries can be a sham. Furthermore, the very notion of 'development' has been corrupted. In many cases, countries have simply been exploited and the majority of their people have become poorer. So, in terms of genuine development, they have gone backwards.

It is against this background that we can understand why there are so many political refugees seeking asylum in 'the West'. A whole criminal industry has grown up around the smuggling of economic refugees across borders, as well as the trafficking of women and children for sexual exploitation.

Exceptions
China and India are notable exceptions to the neo-colonial process I have described. In both of these countries there has been very rapid economic development and both have been able to preserve a real independence. However, the development in these countries has come at the cost of an enormous widening of the gap between the rich and the poor. The rapid development has also caused very serious environmental damage, especially in China. On the credit side, the Chinese people are no longer victims of the periodic famines which they endured in the past.

How is it that China and India have been able to avoid becoming the victims of neo-colonialism? Part of the answer is that both countries have very large populations. This meant that each of them, but especially China, could generate its own process of development without becoming entangled in the Western-dominated system. But size alone would not have saved them from being sucked into the neo-colonial system. The other key factor was that their governments developed policies which ensured their economic independence.

Social Injustice in the West
I have focused on the damaging effects of social injustice in the less developed non-Western countries, because there we see the most glaring examples. Over the past twenty-five years, however, a rather similar form of injustice has expanded in the wealthy Western countries. The result is that the gap between the rich and the poor has widened enormously.

A United Nations study in 2006 found that the richest 2% of adults in the world own more than half the global household wealth. In the USA in 1980 the chief executives of big companies were paid forty-three times as much as the average worker; but by 2005 they were paid over four hundred times as much.[2]

Spirituality?
It may be asked: what has all this to do with spirituality? It is important to insist that, for Christians, spirituality cannot be divorced from morality either at the individual level or in relation to major social and ecological issues. In fact these moral problems are so pervasive and urgent that one would expect that a desire to address them would be part of everybody's deepest concern. To exclude them from one's conception of spirituality – understood as one's deepest heart's desire – means adopting, perhaps even expanding, an enormous blind-spot in one's consciousness.

This raises the further question of why such a blind-spot is so widespread today. How can we explain the fact that millions of copies of hundreds of books about spirituality simply ignore the issues of social injustice and ecological degradation? I think it can be understood at least partly in terms of a combination of self-interest, guilt, and a sense of powerlessness.

The basis for the self-interest is obvious. We middle-class people in the West are among the main beneficiaries of the social injustice and ecological insensitivity which characterise our

2. Klein, *The Shock Doctrine*, p 444.

world. To work for the kind of radical changes which are required goes against our economic interests – at least against our short-term interests.

The influence of guilt is less obvious. However, a little reflection on our own experience will quickly show that guilt, instead of galvanising us to action, tends to paralyse us. Furthermore, it causes us to look for ways of escaping the unpleasant feeling of powerlessness.

It is not surprising that individuals should feel powerless in the face of the global issues of social injustice – even more so than in relation to ecological issues. For it is not so difficult for a person to do something about the environment – for instance, one can refrain from wasting hot water and one can install solar panels. But, how can any individual act effectively to counter the huge disparities of power and wealth in our present-day world?

Ironically, it is this very sense of helplessness which provides the strongest support for continuing injustice. It is in the interests of those in power to convey the impression that the widening gap between the rich and the poor is an inevitable – though perhaps unfortunate – effect of 'the laws of economics'.

It is quite true that the rich-poor gap is widened by economics – provided one is thinking of a particular brand of economics. This is the neo-liberal and monetarist economic theory of what is called 'the Chicago school', associated with the teaching of Milton Friedman and his followers. It is this approach to economics which is at the heart of the neo-conservative agenda in USA and of the neo-liberalism which has been at least partly adopted by the IMF and imposed on very many countries throughout the world.

In the light of all this I have to conclude that a central aspect of any authentic Christian spirituality – and indeed of any truly human spirituality – is a commitment to oppose the imposition of this type of neo-liberal economics at both the national and the international level. A key first step in this opposition is to challenge the assumption that neo-liberalism is the most realistic and effective economic theory for our present-day world. And this involves making a serious effort to understand something about economics and the whole process of economic and social development.

CHAPTER SIXTEEN

A Challenging Spirituality

Those who are interested in a spirituality of social justice need to know something about economics – mainly to enable them to recognise just how uncertain, incomplete, and tentative is the knowledge provided by economic science; and to be able to challenge the assumptions and oversights made by economists.

The science of economics generally takes account only of items that are easily measurable. Economists bridge the gap between their science and the real world by making a whole lot of assumptions. Unfortunately, we often find out too late that the assumptions were unjustified because some key factor had been overlooked.

The most obvious examples can be found in non-Western countries which have set out to be 'developed'. Crucially important factors, with major economic implications, were ignored or played down. For instance, in many cases little or no account was taken of the ways in which the practices and cultural values of non-Western countries differ from those of the West, e.g. the fact that in many African countries the agricultural workers are mainly women rather than men. Furthermore, little account was taken either of the economic effects of the serious social disruption that arises as a result of the extremely rapid growth of the cities or of the economic cost of major problems of security.

However, the biggest mistake was that the (mainly Western) economic advisers to non-Western countries seem to have overlooked the fact that the poorest countries cannot hope to 'develop' in the way the Western countries did. Much of the development of Western countries came though colonisation, which allowed the colonising countries to exploit most of the countries of Latin America, Asia and Africa. But now that the former colonies wish to become 'developed', they have no other set of countries below them to colonise and exploit.

Most of the 'experts' have tacitly ignored the fact that there simply aren't enough resources in our world to enable the poorer countries to be 'developed' in the way development came to the West. Furthermore, it is quite obvious that the rich countries are determined not to give up their disproportionate share of the economic 'cake'. But the 'experts' fail to take account of the limits to available resources.

However, it is not only in non-Western countries that ordinary people have had to pay a high price for the unwarranted omissions or assumptions of economists. Even in the West, many economic 'experts' argue for neo-liberal and monetarist theories which are little more than an ideological justification for policies which favour the rich and make the poor carry the burden of national 'development' or economic 'recovery'. A study of the statistics in Ireland, Britain, and the USA shows that even the partial imposition of this kind of economics has eroded social services and widened the gap between rich and poor.

Probably the most dangerous assumption made by many mainstream economists is that we need set little or no limit to 'economic growth' and to what they call 'production'. They fail to advert to the fact that the 'growth' and 'production' of which they speak is in fact largely a matter of consumption – the using up of precious resources of energy and raw materials, and that it frequently involves polluting the environment as well. It is only in very recent years that economic science has begun to take seriously the whole ecological question.

Unfortunately, most of the economic planners in government service were trained in the older version of economics. All too few of them have undergone the major conversion that is involved in shifting from an uncritical growth-oriented model of economics to one that is more realistic from an ecological point of view. Even fewer of the politicians have been willing to take the risk of moving from short-term populist policies to policies that safeguard the environment and lessen the gap between the rich and the poor at both the national and global levels.

A more realistic science of economics would set out to address some issues which are largely ignored at present. Here are some of the key questions which need to be addressed. What are the long-term economic and social costs of policies which widen the gap between the rich and the poor and create a permanently unemployed under-class, many of whom are very likely to become involved in drugs and crime? How can we ensure that those who introduce new labour-saving technology will have to pay the full social cost and the long-term economic cost of putting people out of work – as well as also paying the full ecological costs of this high-energy technology? What is a realistic price to pay for the consumption of scarce resources of energy and clean water as well as of metals and forests – and to whom and in what form should this price be paid? How best can we work out a proper balance between the economic values of efficiency and such 'soft' values as personal involvement and creativity in work?

Alternatives

The problems and questions in relation to social and ecological injustice are so huge and daunting that those who become aware of them can quickly get discouraged. In order to avoid this kind of paralysis, it is important to move on from identifying the problems to exploring alternatives. Committed Christians may find it helpful to reflect on some texts from the bible which indicate how God inspired the Jews and the early Christians to address these kind of issues.

One of the most striking texts is the one which called on the Israelites to celebrate a 'Jubilee year' every fifty years. This was a year which was designed to close the gap which had opened up in the previous fifty years between the rich and poor:

> In this year all property that has been sold shall be restored to its original owner ... If an Israelite becomes poor and is forced to sell land ... and does not have enough money to buy it back ... it will be returned to its original owner in the next Year of Restoration. (Lev 25:13-28)

This approach may be unrealistic in our modern world– partly because land is no longer the main form of wealth. But in our world the same effect can be achieved by means of a taxation system which effectively redistributes the excess wealth of the rich to the poor. The advantage of such a system is that it can be tailored to produce varying degrees of re-distribution of wealth, through a judicious mix of income taxes, sales taxes, property taxes, and capital gains taxes.

In a democracy, one political party may opt for a quite radical re-distribution of wealth. Their aim will be to provide excellent health and education systems which are available freely to rich and poor alike, together with a whole range of high-quality social security services to cater for those in special need. Meanwhile another political party may adopt a policy of having much lower taxes, thereby leaving a quite wide gap between the rich and the poor in regard to education, health and social services. The choice of which party to put in power is then in the hands of the electorate. Faced with such a choice, one could scarcely claim that one's choice of which party to vote for should be determined by one's economic interests, or by long-standing habit, but not at all by one's spirituality.

Globalisation

In the years after World War II many Western European countries developed systems of social democracy which involved relatively high levels of taxation and were quite effective in redistributing wealth in a realistic way. In more recent years, however, these policies have come under increasing pressure. The countries which had adopted them find themselves almost forced to dismantle their social welfare systems bit by bit, replacing their social democratic systems with a cruder form of capitalism.

One main reason why these countries have been under pressure to allow a widening gap between the rich and the poor is the rapid increase in the process of globalisation. There is nothing wrong in principle with the globalisation process – in fact in many ways it could be a very good thing. The trouble is with the form it has taken in practice. The way it operates at present is that all kinds of manufacturing processes, and services of all kinds (e.g. advisory and support service conducted by phone), have been 'outsourced' to countries where wages are extremely low and where workers are exploited in a variety of other ways.

The result is what has been aptly called 'a race to the bottom'. What this means is that middle-class and lower-class workers in the more developed world – particularly those in the social democracies of western Europe – find themselves faced with a choice between increasing unemployment or lower wages and greater pressures in the workplace. This in turn means that less tax-money is available for the provision of a high level of health and social services.

Ironically, this 'race to the bottom' is accompanied by what might be called 'a race to the top' by transnational companies and those in top management roles in big business. The top executives of these companies earn ever higher salaries as well as major bonuses and perks of all kinds. Furthermore, globalisation allows the companies to greatly increase their profits by ensuring that these profits are, theoretically but legally, earned mainly in 'tax haven' countries where little or no tax has to be paid.

One might wonder why, in the case of large corporations, 'the race to the bottom' is replaced by a 'race to the top' – in sharp contrast to what happens in the case of ordinary workers. Why is it that worldwide competition for the top jobs does not drive down the salaries of these top executives? Why is it that those who are 'head-hunted' to take on the top positions are offered huge incentives to do so?

The explanation is twofold. Firstly, there is a rather closed self-interested circle of people at the top of the business world where decisions about salaries are made. It is in the interests of all in that group to ensure that the salaries of top executives and directors are kept high – and in fact are constantly being increased. Secondly, the directors of these companies know that even the enormous salaries paid to those at the top are relatively insignificant compared to the far greater profits that can be generated by highly-paid, ruthless and efficient chief executives.

The obvious conclusion from all this is that anybody who wishes to develop an authentically Christian spirituality which is fully realistic must make a serious effort to understand the process of globalisation and must seek ways of overcoming its negative effects. It is clear that these negative effects cannot be eliminated if people's efforts to do so are confined to working at the national level. The problems are global and so they must be tackled at the global level.

But how can these global problems be addressed? There is

need for well-organised action at several levels. First of all, committed people in the West ought to put pressure on their own governments to work through the United Nations for universally binding conventions which will put an end to tax havens and will protect both the environment and workers' rights all over the world. Secondly, there is need for a strong and independent trade union movement in countries like China, India, and the other (mainly Asian) countries to which work is being outsourced. In practice, this means that there is need for powerful international trade union federations to give support to the emerging trade union movement in the countries where workers are poorly paid and treated badly.

A Community Spirituality

All this takes us a long way from the highly individualistic conception of spirituality which is so common in the West today. It may even, at first sight, seem a long way from the bible. But the spirituality of the bible is not one that can be adopted by an isolated individual. It is above all a community spirituality.

In biblical times communities were local and to some extent national; there was little or no sense of a worldwide human community. But in our time, with the rapid development of 'the global village' – through communications, economics, and ecology – we have to think of the whole human race as the primary community. The response of people all over the world to such natural disasters as earthquakes and tsunamis shows that we already have an emerging global concern. This needs to be built on and given a more overtly political orientation. In that process we can draw on the spirituality of liberation which has been one of the most important developments in Christianity in recent times. I shall develop this point further in the next chapter.

In the meantime we can turn to the New Testament. There we find some particularly interesting texts about the economic life of a community. The most radical text is where Jesus says that those who are materially poor are especially privileged. They are 'blessed' or 'happy' because they share in the new Realm of God (Lk 6:20). Jesus is not saying that the poor are morally better than others. The point is rather that those who are poor or despised are the ones most in need of his good news –

and are also the ones most likely to be open to it. The liberating words and actions of Jesus are designed to bring those who have been marginalised back into the mainstream of human society.

Another striking passage is the story Jesus told about the eleventh hour labourer (Mt 20:1-16). This man, who worked for only the final hour of the day, is paid the same amount as those who worked all day. If we try to see what lesson this parable is teaching us for today's world, perhaps we should see it as suggesting that a worker should not be penalised for failing to find employment.

But how did the early Christians try to put the values of Jesus into practice in their everyday life? There are two passages in the Acts of the Apostles (Acts 2:44-5 and 4:32-5) which indicate that the members of the Christian community in the Jerusalem area had a quite radical way of ensuring that nobody was left in poverty. They shared their belongings with each other, distributing them according to the need of each person.

This practice of a total sharing of goods has not endured in the church – except among the members of religious communities who take vows. However, down through the ages the followers of Jesus have always felt called to be generous in sharing with each other, above all with those who have special needs. The sharing of resources remains essential in this world where resources are spread so unevenly and unfairly. And it is helpful to broaden our understanding of the word 'resources'. Sometimes it may be more important to give time to others than to give them money or food. And it seems particularly important nowadays that we share our hope for, and belief in, a more just and humane world – and our commitment to work and struggle for it, even when that hope is dismissed by others as quite unrealistic.

What emerges from a reading of the New Testament is that an isolated individual cannot practice a truly Christian spirituality. The challenge for us is to develop and live out a spirituality which is both community-oriented and also strongly counter-cultural. This means in practice that we have to take very seriously two distinct conceptions of community. On the one hand we need to look outward, recognising that we are members of the wider community that is humanity as a whole. But at the same time we need the support of a much smaller group of like-minded people. If we cannot find such a group we need to set about trying to establish one – a group of friends and colleagues whose spirituality gives a central place to a commitment to bring about radical changes in the political, economic, social, and cultural structures of our present-day globalised world.

CHAPTER SEVENTEEN

A Spirituality of Liberation
and Reconciliation

In the New Testament, Jesus insists that he is to be recognised in the poor, the sick, and the prisoners (Mt 25:35-6). This text lies at the very heart of liberation spirituality. It is an approach which complements and at the same time challenges mainstream Western spirituality. It does so by inviting us to take more account of the experience the poor of our world. The phrase 'the poor' here refers not just to those who have little or no money but also to racial or ethnic minorities, people who are subjected to prejudice because of their sexual orientation, and marginalised groups of all kinds.

Central to liberation spirituality is a realisation that God has a special concern for the poor and the marginalised. Those who adopt this spirituality are convinced that it is not enough for privileged people to see 'the poor' as objects of their compassion. They are inspired by this statement of St Paul: 'God chose those who by human standards ... are weak to shame the strong, those who by human standards are common and contemptible, indeed those who count for nothing, to reduce to nothing all those that do count for something ...' (1 Cor 1:27-8). Consequently, they borrow a phrase used by Pope John Paul II during a visit to Latin America and say that the poor are 'the favourites of God'. Not only that, but they believe that the poor are also a channel of revelation – meaning that God uses them to teach us lessons about God and the world which we would not otherwise hear.

The spirituality of liberation has by now flourished in the church – or at least in some parts of the church – for forty years. It first came into prominence in 1968, when the Latin American bishops, gathered at Medellín, saw the problems of poverty, injustice and oppression as 'signs of the times'. The bishops interpreted these problems as a call from God's Spirit to follow Jesus by being in solidarity with the poor and the oppressed in their struggle against poverty and injustice.

The many committed Christians who have answered this call and spread it to other parts of the world believe that the poor, the marginalised, and the disadvantaged are privileged instruments of God in carrying through the saving work of Jesus. Furthermore, they are convinced that the poor and the disadvantaged have a privileged role in reading 'the signs of the times'. They believe that if we read these signs through the eyes of the poor we will read them more correctly and more adequately than we otherwise would.

If we do not read 'the signs of the times' through the eyes of the poor, much of our work to promote the reign of God in the world will be misguided and defective. Furthermore, if theologians and church leaders do not take sufficient account of the perspective of the poor, even the guidance given to Christians in the form of the official social teaching of the church will be incomplete and imperfect – and may perhaps even at times lead people astray. At first sight this may seem to be an over-statement, but a little reflection on some of the serious mistakes made by church leaders in the past will show that it is not an exaggeration. For instance, Pope Pius IX condemned democracy. And right up to the time John XXIII issued his encyclical *Mater et Magistra* in 1961, the popes and most Catholic Church leaders were very reluctant to approve of a comprehensive system of social welfare benefits provided by the State.

As we look back on forty years of commitment by Christians who have struggled and suffered for human liberation and social justice, we can see that experience as a deeply spiritual one, one where God has been truly present. The spirituality of liberation has offered to the mainstream church, and to the wider human society, new insight into how poor people experience themselves and their world – and, perhaps more importantly, how they experience God. This spirituality throws light on an aspect of our Christian faith which had largely been neglected in the past, namely, how God is present and active in the world through the struggle of the poor to survive and to overcome social injustice and oppression.

Social Conditioning and 'Signs of the Times'

There is a further reason for giving a special weight to the experience of those who are poor or powerless. It is that people who are wealthy and powerful – or privileged in any other way – tend to assume that they are more well-informed than others. Their privileged position inclines them to imagine that those who are poor and powerless, or who do not have much formal education, are less intelligent and have a very inadequate grasp of what is happening in society. When writing about the 'signs of the times' in Chapter 6, I noted that people's prejudices can influence how they interpret these signs. A prime example of such prejudice is the assumption by many upper and middle class people that they know better than the poor what is good for society – and even for the poor themselves. This kind of group prejudice is an example of what I would call 'cultural arrogance'.

The way we understand what is happening in our world is very influenced by our social circumstances. If we are born into a wealthy and powerful family or social class we are very likely to take on the assumptions and prejudices of the people around us. On the other hand, if we are born and grow up in a family or social class that is poor, or that is part of an oppressed or marginalised minority, we are likely to read the scene through very different eyes.

Some years ago I had an experience which brought this home to me in a very vivid way. I was taking part in a pilgrimage in which a mixed group of nomadic 'Travellers' and 'settled people' were walking across Ireland to visit a shrine on a sacred mountain in Connemara. On the first night, shortly after we had stopped to pitch our tents and park our caravans, the local Gardaí (police) arrived to tell us brusquely that we could not camp in that area. However, as soon as they became aware that some of our group were priests and members of religious communities their whole tone changed; now we were welcome to camp there. This made me realise that the normal experience which Travellers have of the police is a far less pleasant one than mine. Consequently, I had to revise my assumption that the police are generally polite and friendly to everybody except when they are being attacked or abused. This experience caused me to really 'let in' a reality which

I had previously been only vaguely aware of: that Travellers, and others who are marginalised in our society, are often treated harshly by those in positions of authority.

Any serious examination of the concept 'reading the signs of the times' needs to take particular account of the fact that the 'reading' gets distorted by our socially conditioned assumptions or prejudices about the world and about ourselves. Unfortunately, most of the articulate church people who take it on themselves to 'read' these signs are themselves rather privileged people. Consequently, it is quite likely that they have unconsciously taken on some of the assumptions and prejudices of the privileged classes and groups in our society. One of the main aims of a spirituality of liberation is to correct the misreading of the signs which may arise from these prejudices or unquestioned assumptions.

In order to compensate for the 'blind spot' in the thinking of privileged groups, it is necessary to pay particular attention to the experience of those who are less privileged. As I noted when writing about Moses in Chapter 8 above, privileged people who wish to help the poor must first of all be in solidarity with them at an experiential level. This sharing of the experience of those who are disadvantaged needs to come before one is in a position to help them effectively. It may then lead on to action in the form of an option for and with the poor.

Working with the Poor

Less privileged people may well find it hard to articulate their experience – and particularly hard to do so in the kind of language that can be heard by the rich and the powerful. The ideal solution to that difficulty is not to have some more privileged person speak on their behalf. It is rather to empower poor or disadvantaged people to find their own voice. Having done so, the would-be helper may eventually be able to come *with* them as they demand their rights, rather than simply speaking or acting *on their behalf*.[1] That is a crucial element in the spirituality of liberation.

1. I have treated this topic in some detail, with numerous practical examples, in a long chapter which I contributed to the book *Scrutinizing the Signs of the Times in the Light of the Gospel*, edited by Johan Verstraeten, Peeters, (Leuven/Louvain, 2007) pp 247-272.

Consequently, those of us who take on this spirituality are committed to finding ways to be in solidarity with the poor and disadvantaged at an experiential level. Following on from that it means we must learn how to be silent for much of the time in order to *listen deeply* to what the poor are saying and feeling. Furthermore, it means we need to learn how to *facilitate* groups, either informally or formally, in articulating their feelings, their experiences, their convictions, and what they want to say to those in power.

Adopting a spirituality of liberation also leads us to reject the kind of pious neutrality – even indifference – in regard to politics which is not uncommon in people who wish to develop their spirituality. In other words, it involves recognising that spirituality is not just a private affair, a one-to-one relationship with God. Spirituality has also a public, even political, dimension. If we ignore that, our spirituality will be seriously defective. On the other hand, if we take seriously the public dimension, and particularly if we look at what is happening in the world from the perspective of the poor and the underprivileged, then our relationship with God and with others will be enormously enriched. Furthermore, we will recognise 'signs of the times' which we would otherwise miss. And we will have a far better chance of interpreting correctly what God is saying to us through these signs.

Reconciliation
Reconciliation is the restoration of good relations between individuals, or groups, or whole nations. A first important point about it is that the achievement of liberation does not yet mean that the wounds of the past have been healed. So liberation should ideally lead on to reconciliation, since liberation otherwise remains incomplete. That is why I have put both topics in this one chapter. I have written at some length elsewhere about reconciliation,[2] so I shall be rather brief in my treatment of the topic here.

Because I have been dealing in this chapter and the previous one with large-scale social justice, I shall focus here mainly on

2. *Mission in Today's World*, Dublin (Columba Press: 2000) and Maryknoll (Orbis: 2000), pp 128-143.

reconciliation between very large groups – for instance, between people of colour and 'white people' in South Africa or in the USA. However, we must recognise that even when this kind of political reconciliation has been successful, this still leaves millions of people with the scars of the oppression which they have suffered. These people still need some form of more personal reconciliation and healing.

It is important also to distinguish between two different situations where political reconciliation is needed. One is where a struggle or war has taken place between two sides which are fairly evenly matched – for instance, the fighting between the Serbs and the Croats in the 1990s. The other is the situation where an oppressed group, such as the African and so-called 'coloured' people in South Africa, have struggled for justice and have eventually succeeded.

A key point – one which is particularly relevant in the case of past oppression – is that reconciliation is not a substitute for the restoration of justice. It is a fundamental mistake to try to rush into it too quickly. Before people attempt to move into a process of reconciliation, it is necessary that the injuries of the past be named and acknowledged, and at least the more gross injustices be eliminated and fundamental justice be established.

Nevertheless, a certain amount of realism is called for. Where a whole ethnic group has been oppressed and exploited for centuries, as happened in South Africa, in Ireland, and in almost all colonial situations, reconciliation should ideally involve reparation for the accumulated injuries and injustices of the past. But in practice most oppressed groups do not demand such an exact accounting. They are generally willing to settle for equality in the present, together with some significant efforts towards restoring the balance. One element in this might be heavy taxation of those who have benefitted from the past injustices. A further element might be a limited amount of reverse discrimination in state appointments, so as to give a proportion of those who been oppressed an opportunity to break into areas of work from which they had been excluded.

A Gift from God
From the point of view of spirituality, a central aspect of recon-

ciliation is that it is experienced as a gift from God. Of course people have to work for it, and have to accept and welcome it when it comes. But when it does take place, there seems to be a certain gratuitous quality to it. The Christian will see God's hand as particularly evident in bringing about the element of forgiveness which is so vital in any reconciliation. The hurts of the past run so deep that it is extremely difficult for the person who has been hurt to truly forgive the other, through human efforts alone. When forgiveness comes, it often comes as an answer to prayer, perhaps at an unexpected time and bringing with it an experience of deep spiritual freedom.

In many cases reconciliation goes further than people would have expected. In the 1990s, people in South Africa and all over the world were moved by the remarkable generosity with which Nelson Mandela reached out to the people who had oppressed his people for centuries. His graciousness did much to ease the tensions of the transition and to inspire people on either side to move towards real reconciliation.

A more recent example is the way in which, in Northern Ireland in 2007, Ian Paisley and Martin McGuinness came to work so closely together and with so much tolerant good humour that people dubbed them 'The Chuckle Brothers'. Of course most of us do not know to what extent this public display of ease and warmth was mirrored at the more personal level. But, even if there was still a legacy of interpersonal dislike and distrust between them, their ability to model congenial co-operation in public made a vital contribution towards reconciliation and could be experienced as a gift of grace.

Healing the Wounds
One of the most damaging effects of long-standing oppression and injustice is that the victims tend to internalise the oppression. In other words, they come to imagine that they are somehow responsible for what is happening to them, and even that they deserve it. Furthermore, the victims, in order to survive, may have blocked out of their consciousness some or all of the hurt and damage inflicted on them. People in that situation may have to engage in quite a lot of counselling or therapeutic work in order to bring their hurt and anger into the full light of con-

sciousness and eventually move on into genuine freedom of spirit.

One effective way in which the healing of past hurts can be brought about is through some public or semi-public ritual. The ritual may be a way of expressing feelings and commitments which are too deep and complex to be put into words. The formality of the ritual may offer oppressor and victim a safe way to come together without running the risk of re-opening old wounds.

Reconciliation does not remove the injuries and wounds of the past. It is not a question of going back to the situation that existed prior to the oppression. What we must look for instead is something quite new – a state, perhaps, where both the repentant oppressor and the newly healed victim may now become 'wounded healers' who work separately or together to bring reconciliation to others.

CHAPTER EIGHTEEN

A Spirituality for Sellers and Buyers

One of the pleasures which tourists in Africa and Asia experience is shopping in the open-air markets which are so common in those parts of the world. I want to suggest that there is an implicit spirituality which governs how these markets work – a spirituality or ethos which has much to teach people of the Western world. Those of us who grew up perhaps sixty years ago in rural parts of Ireland or other Western countries may recall that much the same ethos applied there – it governed everything from selling a pair of shoes in a local shop to buying a cow at the cattle-fair.

Needless to say, the ethos and spirituality of the street-market is not entirely different from the ethos of the modern business world. A central point in each case is that both the buyer and the seller are aiming to complete the transaction at what each of them considers to be 'a good price'. However, there are also significant differences. Buying and selling in the street-market or traditional village are regulated by additional values and priorities which are given less priority in the modern business world.

The most important of these extra values is respect. The seller soon becomes aware of the attitude of the tourist who is a would-be buyer. If the seller feels insulted by brusqueness or arrogance on the part of the buyer, or thinks that the only aim of the tourist is to beat the seller down to the last cent, then the transaction may fall through. Street-market sellers are interested in establishing a personal relationship with the customer. If it emerges that the buyer is not interested in such a relationship and is concerned only with the object and the price, then the seller is likely to reciprocate by seeking to take advantage of the buyer. But if the would-be buyer shows respect and sensitivity by taking time to admire the merchandise and make small talk, then seller and buyer can go on to engage in the subtle 'game' of bargaining.

Success in the bargaining game is not defined in purely economic terms. Of course the seller and the buyer must eventually agree on the price. But, equally important, each should come out of the 'game' with the satisfaction of feeling respected by the other. They must feel: 'This is somebody with whom I enjoy doing business and with whom I am willing to do business again.' If they establish a really warm relationship, the seller may give the buyer a gift or offer an unusually good bargain. On the other hand, buyers who come to admire and like the seller may feel unusually generous and so may not beat the price down as much as they otherwise would.

Some foreign tourists come to the market stall with an attitude that is entirely mercenary and calculating. In that case they will interpret the 'special offers' and the various other nuances of the bargaining game in narrowly economic terms. By adopting this attitude they become like an over-competitive football player who is determined to win at all costs and never thinks of enjoying the game as a game.

On the other hand, those who willingly enter into the bargaining game, know that 'success' is not defined in purely economic terms. For those who really engage in that game, 'success' includes the excitement of wrestling with the seller and making use of such acceptable ploys as pretending to walk away. But they know that the rules of the game demand that they do not insult or exploit the seller. A really successful outcome will result in a genuinely interpersonal relationship between the two parties. They may even become good friends. But there is no naïveté on either side. Part of the respect each of them has for the other is admiration for the other's shrewdness in gaining a good bargain.

Spirituality

What has all this to do with spirituality? I suggest that the ethos or 'rules of the game' which govern human relationships in the street market are implicitly a practical spirituality which is lived out in everyday life. They enable people to live together in harmony and mutual respect. At their best they foster a real sense of community and the development of warm interpersonal relationships between all the people involved.

The key to all this is that the street-market ethos or implicit spirituality situates people's economic relationships within the context of a much broader set of human relationships and values. It leaves space for the mixture of motives with which sellers and buyers operate. It is not so unrealistic as to assume that people always act on the basis of altruistic motives. But it provides an ambience where a reasonable degree of self-interest fits comfortably with respect for others and with congeniality, friendship, and a sense of community.

The Business World

This is in sharp contrast to the business ethos which has developed in the Western world over the past couple of hundred years. That business world seems to have cut itself off to a considerable extent from the wider context of relationships where people relate to each other in a humane and respectful manner. It seems to be assumed that the activity of buying and selling is governed by different norms, and operates on the basis of values which are significantly different from those which apply in other areas of life. 'The world of business' appears to have its own ethos and its own ethics – ones which in some respects are inimical to the values which make us fully human and which are characteristic of any civilised society. Business people in the West seem to have carved out a special sphere of life where self-interest takes precedence over all other values.

Idealistic people may be tempted to criticise this world of business to a point where they are simply presenting a caricature. It is important to avoid such exaggeration. We have to acknowledge that many of those who work in the world of business feel quite uneasy about the direction it has taken, and are trying to change it.

Furthermore, some very wealthy business people have become philanthropists and in doing so have brought major benefits to human society. One thinks, for instance, of the Nobel peace prize and the other Nobel prizes. Another example is the Cadbury Foundation which supports care for older people; it was set up in line with Quaker values. One might also mention the Ford Foundation and the Bill Gates and Warren Buffet Foundation. Even more striking is the almost secret philanthropy of a Chuck Feeney who does not even want his own name to be associated with the huge sums of money which he gives to deserving causes.

In principle, there is a clear distinction between high-minded philanthropy and sponsorship of festivals, sports events, etc. Sponsorship is by no means disinterested: it is a way of advertising or of PR (public relations) which is intended to contribute in the long run to the profits of the company by keeping the brand-name in the public eye. However, in more recent years there seems to be a tendency to blur the distinction between philanthropy and PR. Perhaps this is an indication of the extent to which practically every activity of a business enterprise is evaluated almost entirely in economic terms. Outings for employees, gifts for customers, benefits provided to the local community – all these are seen as contributing to 'the bottom line' which is increased profits.

The mentality which I am describing is evident most obviously in those in management and accountancy roles. But, more and more, this 'business ethic' is being imposed on the ordinary employees. They find their contribution to the enterprise being assessed again and again almost exclusively in terms of the extent to which their work contributes to increased profits for the company. They are very aware that the project may be 'downsized', or the work they are doing may be 'contracted out'; and so they may lose their jobs. This uncertainty puts them under great stress. It also generates a spirit of competition between the workers – and this undermines the sense of community.

It is interesting to note that what we might call 'the mercenary mentality' has also fed back into local communities. They now feel entitled to demand their 'pound of flesh' from any business enterprise which is located in their area. It is as though the creation of a sense of community between the business and the community were secondary, almost accidental.

Can it be Changed?

An increasing number of people are waking up to the fact that this modern business ethic is doing great damage to people and communities. Many people would like to re-humanise the business world. The aim would be that, at a minimum, there would be genuine respect for the workers, the suppliers, the customers or clients, and even for those involved in competing businesses. Hopefully, this could lead on to the development of a strong sense of community and the growth of warm personal relationships between many of the people involved. In other words, the world of business would no longer be governed by just the dominant values of efficiency and profitability. Instead, it would be animated by the mixture of values which is typical of human behaviour at its best in other spheres of life such as home-life, or the academic world, or recreation.

If this ideal were achieved what would, in effect, have emerged would be a genuine spirituality of the business world. This spirituality would replace the one-dimensional, competitive and exploitative set of attitudes which seem so dominant at present. However, the creation of such an authentic spirituality of business comes up against serious obstacles.

First of all, the present-day economic system operates at a global level. Work can be out-sourced to countries where wages are minimal, where workers have little or no rights, and where environmental concern has a very low priority. This gives rise to a 'dog-eat-dog' atmosphere where companies which have more enlightened policies can quickly be put out of business. As I noted in a previous chapter, it also means that workers are at the mercy of 'a race to the bottom'. This is because employers, in order to stay in business, have to pay their employees less and less, and to put them under ever greater pressures.

Furthermore, workers in poor countries, and the poor countries themselves, find themselves trapped in this exploitative system. The present policies and rules of trade imposed by the International Monetary Fund and the World Trade Organisation, and by the banking system in the wealthy countries, make it difficult if not impossible for them to break out of the poverty trap.

The globalised economic system is also backed up by political and military power. Politicians are supported – sometimes bribed – by wealthy corporations to further their interests. Lobbyists are employed by these companies to put pressure on people in government to adopt policies which favour big business. At the international level, poorer countries which 'get out of line' are compelled by increasing degrees of force to acquiesce in their role as suppliers of cheap labour and raw materials.

Finally, there is what we might call an ideological super-structure which purports to justify the present business world model. Basically, this is the theory that there are strict 'laws of economics' which ensure that the system works efficiently. A central tenet of this economic theory is in fact a quite unwarranted assumption. It is that when each person is free to act to further his or her own self-interest, this somehow adds up to a situation in which the needs of all are met effectively and efficiently.

There is ample evidence in today's world to show that, quite frequently, the common good is by no means the end result of a situation where everybody is motivated solely by self-interest. One might, for instance, think of how commonages frequently get over-grazed. Again, one can see how today's fishing-fleets are wiping out the fish-stocks of the oceans of the world.

Furthermore, it is clear that the 'laws' of economics are not in fact allowed to operate in an unfettered way. There is gross interference by powerful countries and corporations in the way countries and companies and individuals trade with each other. So-called 'free trade' is applied quite selectively, being invoked only in situations where it suits the rich and the powerful.

We must also add that, despite the theory that self-interest is the key to effective economics, the reality is that concern for the community does in fact sometimes influence the way important economic decisions are made. Not only that, but there is also respectable research which shows that, in making economic decisions, people quite frequently are influenced by interpersonal relationships rather than solely by self-interest and narrowly economic considerations.[1]

An Alternative?

Some would claim that it is quite unrealistic even to try to replace the present dominant business ethos with a more respectful and humane ethos and spirituality. Certainly, it will not be easy to do so. But committed believers, buoyed up by hope, can and must tackle this task. In order to have any serious prospect of success it is necessary to address the problem at the economic level, at the political level, and at the ideological level.

Nowadays there are serious economic arguments which can

---

1. For instance, Benedetto Gui, 'Beyond Transactions: On the Interpersonal Dimension of Economic Reality', *Annals of Public and Cooperative Economics* 71:2 (June 2000): 139-170. Also, Bruno Frey, *Not Just for the Money: An Economic Theory of Personal Motivation* (Edward Elgar, Cheltenham UK, Northampton MA, USA: 1998).

be used to challenge the dominant mentality. Perhaps the most obvious of these is the ecological argument: one or two particular individuals can get away with acting on the basis of narrow self-interest while ignoring the damage they are doing to the environment; but if a very large number do so, then everybody suffers. There are also a growing number of business people who are taking account of values which go beyond self-interest. These are 'soft values' such as the promotion of creativity, teamwork, and a sense of community in the workplace.[2]

At the political level, we find many idealistic groups who have been remarkably successful in using publicity campaigns and boycotts to put pressure on companies which exploit people or the environment. The success of these campaigns gives hope to idealists that much more can be done – provided people of goodwill can be organised to increase the pressure on big business.

There have also been some successes at the inter-governmental level. Under the auspices of the United Nations, most countries have adopted various conventions which put limits to narrow self-interest – for instance, 'The Kyoto Protocol' in relation to climate change and 'The Convention on the Law of the Sea' which puts some limits on the exploitation of the sea-bed. Furthermore, there is the successful outcome of the Montreal Protocol of 1987 through which countries drastically cut the use of the chemical compounds used in fridges and propellants, which were doing so much damage to the ozone layer.

Further success depends largely on increased public awareness and pressure on governments 'from the ground up'. For instance, there is an on-going campaign for the introduction of what has come to be called 'the Tobin Tax'. It would involve restricting the short-term speculation in currencies which does such damage to national economies.[3]

This brings us to the ideological level. Here we are dealing not with outward changes in practices or laws but with the

2. I have written about this in more detail in *The Spirituality of Leadership*, pp 62-4 and 69-71 (US edition *Faith at Work*, pp 49-51 and 56-8).
3. For a further list of practical proposals for change which would make the international system more just and transparent, see Joseph E. Stiglitz, *Making Globalization Work*, London (Allen Lane, Penguin: 2006) pp 155-9.

mentality of people. It is obvious, of course, that people's mind-set and attitudes would be very different from the present if there were widespread acceptance of the kind of values we have looked at throughout this book. But the question is: how can such a change of mentality be fostered? I can think of three ways of doing so.

First of all – and perhaps most importantly – when groups of committed people live by these values they model the kind of society which is possible. There are many families and religious or spiritual communities who endeavour to do so. Committed groups in several countries make use of 'alternative money' such as the 'lets trading system', for the exchange of goods and services.[4] Individuals and communities who live on the basis of a spirituality which espouses counter-cultural values, not only survive but can actually thrive and live a rich and fulfilled human life. This amounts to a strong argument in favour of adopting such a spirituality.

Following on from that, committed people can seek to influence others through public awareness programmes. One of the key aims of such programmes is to remind people that they are not just helpless victims of the present system. Change is possible, and awareness-raising campaigners have succeeded in recent years in making the general public conscious of the urgency of several issues. They have been fairly successful in their campaigns on environmental issues such as global warming and damage to the ozone layer.

Working for change, either in legislation or in public awareness, is generally a slow process. It is only quite rarely that dramatic breakthroughs occur. But that is no reason for giving up hope.

It is also possible to work with business-people themselves – helping them to find ways to break out of the trap in which they find themselves. There have been some reasonably successful efforts to do this. For instance, some years ago a group of prominent business people came together in what was called 'The Caux Roundtable'. There they established guiding principles which would make for a more responsible and respectful business ethic. However, these do not go far enough. There is need

4. See http://www.gmlets.u-net.com/faq.html#whatis

for much more; and there is an opening for it, because many people in the business world are now searching for a spirituality which will sustain and nourish them.[5]

Religion and Spirituality

The great world religions, at their best, provide valuable insight about the kind of changes that are required. At the same time they offer inspiration and energy to those who long for a more respectful and humane business ethos. They provide their adherents with a set of values which challenge the present business ethos.

Unfortunately, however, many members of these religions often fail to implement these values in their everyday lives. This seems to be particularly true in the area of business. Far too many people seem to assume that religion and spirituality are concerned with the private and interpersonal aspects of life but not with the spheres of business and politics.

In this situation there is need for urgent action by those of us who seek to be committed religious people. We need to move deep into the heart of our own religions, focusing on the life-giving values we find there. Have located these values, we must live by them and share them with other people, rather than concentrating on the more external aspects of our religion. In doing this we can make common cause with the many people – including people in the world of business – who are uneasy with the word 'religion' but are searching for a fully rounded and satisfying spirituality.

We who believe that our religion, at its best, provides us with a truly deep and comprehensive spirituality must be willing, at times, to hold back. We must not imagine that offering quick solutions based on our own religious beliefs will provide an easy answer to the searchings of others. Rather, we need to remind ourselves that the Spirit is at work in the hearts of all. Trusting the Spirit, we can afford to be patient, while encouraging our non-religious friends and colleagues to search for a spirituality which meets their deepest heart's desire.

5. For a more extended treatment of this whole topic see my chapter, entitled 'Alternative Business Ethics: A Challenge for Leadership', pp 211-228, in Gabriel Flynn (ed), *Leadership and Business Ethics*, Springer, 2008.